Why things don't work
TRAIN

www.raintreepublishers.co.uk
Visit our website to find out more information about Raintree books.

To order:
☎ Phone 44 (0) 1865 888112
▤ Send a fax to 44 (0) 1865 314091
▢ Visit the Raintree bookshop at www.raintreepublishers.co.uk to browse
our catalogue and order online.

Why things don't work TRAIN
was produced by

David West 👥 Children's Books
7 Princeton Court
55 Felsham Road
London SW15 1AZ

Editor: Dominique Crowley
Consultant: David T. Wright

First published in Great Britain by
Raintree, Halley Court, Jordan Hill, Oxford OX2 8EJ, part of
Harcourt Education. Raintree is a registered trademark of Harcourt
Education Ltd.

10 digit ISBN: 1 4062 0548 6
13 digit ISBN: 978 1 4062 0548 0

11 10 09 08 07
10 9 8 7 6 5 4 3 2 1

British Library Cataloguing in Publication Data

West, David
 Train. - (Why things don't work)
 1.Locomotives - Maintenance and repair - Comic books,
 strips, etc. - Juvenile literature 2.Railroads - Trains -
 Comic books, strips, etc. - Juvenile literature
 I.Title
 625.2'6'0288

Printed and bound in China

Why things don't work

TRAIN

by David West

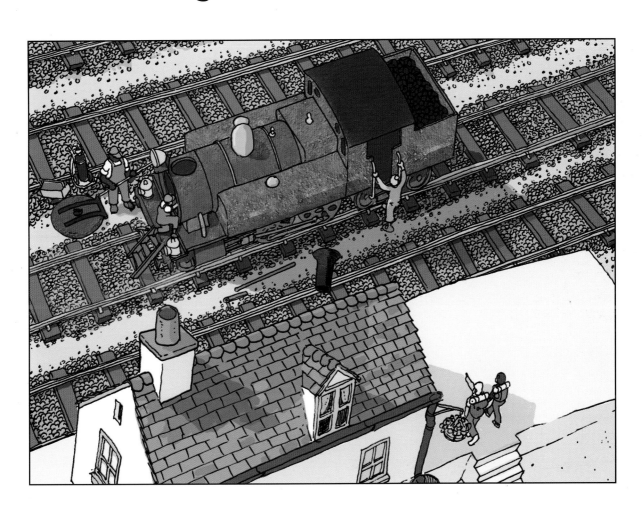

Contents

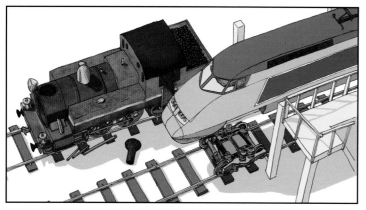

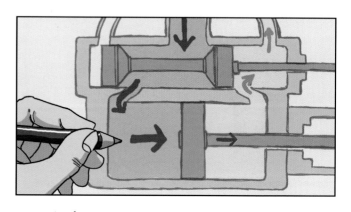
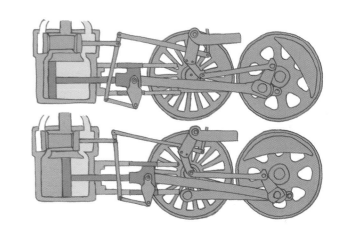

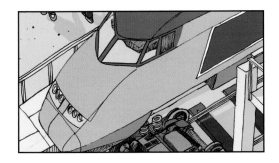

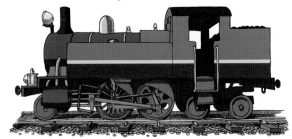

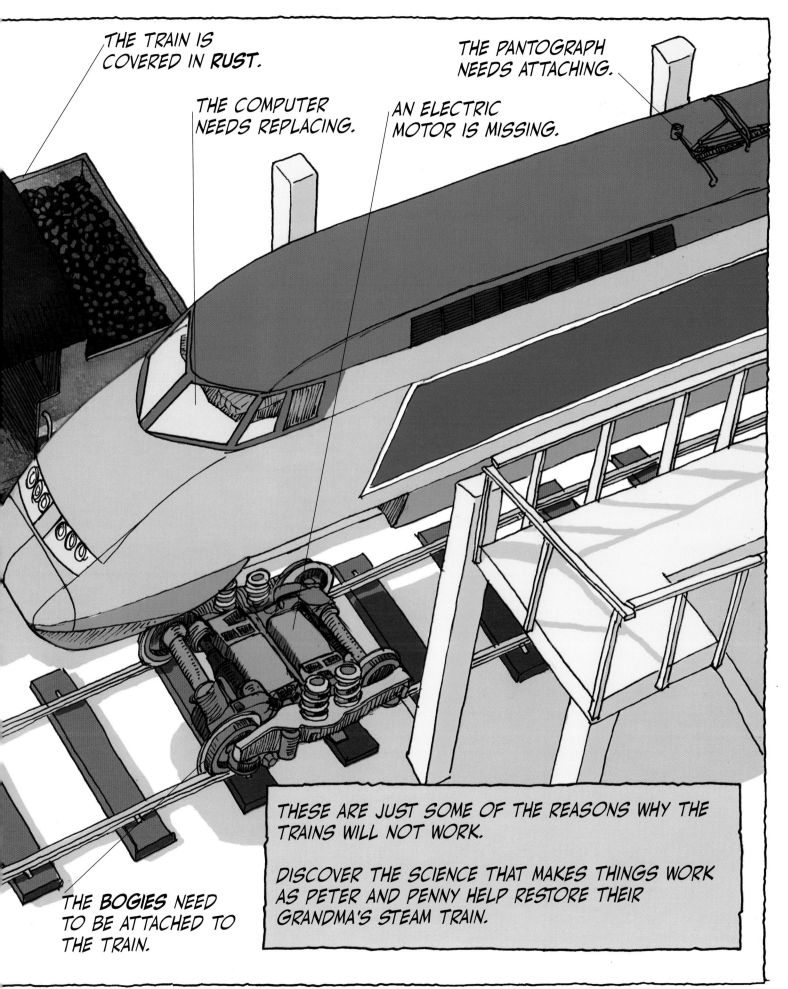

7

PETER AND PENNY ARRIVE AT GRANDMA'S TRAIN MUSEUM.

WOW! THIS PLACE IS AMAZING.

THERE'S GRANDMA LIZZIE.

OVER HERE, KIDS.

YOU'VE ARRIVED JUST IN TIME TO HELP WITH MY TANK ENGINE.

LET'S PUT YOUR BAGS IN THE STATION HOUSE.

THESE CARRY HEAT AND SMOKE THROUGH THE BOILER, FROM THE **FIREBOX** AT THE OTHER END.

THE SMOKE IS DRAWN OUT THROUGH THE CHIMNEY.

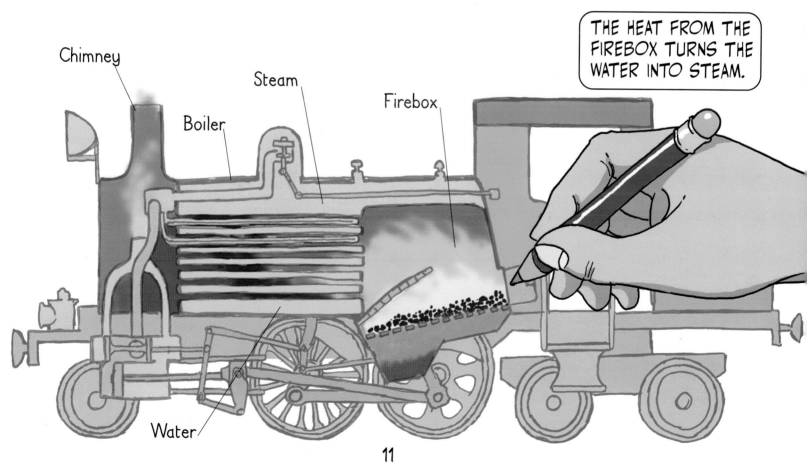

Chimney

Boiler

Steam

Firebox

Water

THE HEAT FROM THE FIREBOX TURNS THE WATER INTO STEAM.

AS THE WATER TURNS TO STEAM, IT BUILDS UP PRESSURE.

THIS IS BECAUSE STEAM (A GAS) TAKES UP MORE SPACE THAN WATER (A LIQUID).

Steam

Boiling water (100°C)

Heat

BUT THE STEAM IS NOT ALLOWED TO EXPAND UNTIL IT HAS BUILT UP ENOUGH PRESSURE. THEN IT HAS THE POWER TO MOVE THINGS, JUST LIKE THE LID OFF A SAUCEPAN.

Steam

Boiling water

Heat

THIS GAUGE, HERE, SHOWS THE PRESSURE. WHEN THE STEAM GETS TO A HIGH ENOUGH PRESSURE, IT CAN BE PIPED TO THE PISTONS.

YOU CAN SEE THE PISTONS ARE AT THE FRONT. THEY ARE ON EACH SIDE OF THE TRAIN.

13

AS YOU CAN SEE, THERE ARE TWO PISTONS IN EACH CYLINDER CASING.

HOW DO THEY WORK?

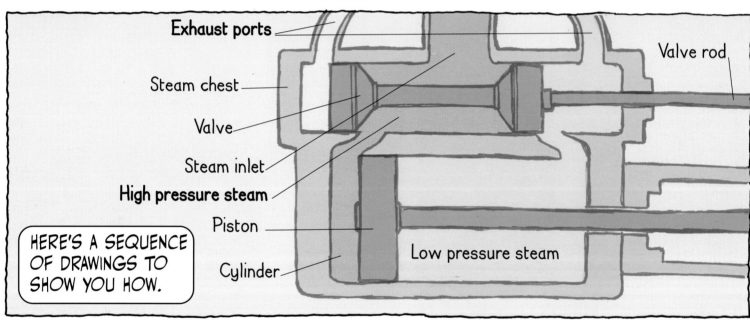

Exhaust ports

Valve rod

Steam chest

Valve

Steam inlet

High pressure steam

Piston

Cylinder

Low pressure steam

HERE'S A SEQUENCE OF DRAWINGS TO SHOW YOU HOW.

HIGH PRESSURE STEAM FROM THE BOILER ENTERS THE CYLINDER THROUGH THE INLET. AS IT EXPANDS IT PUSHES THE PISTON.

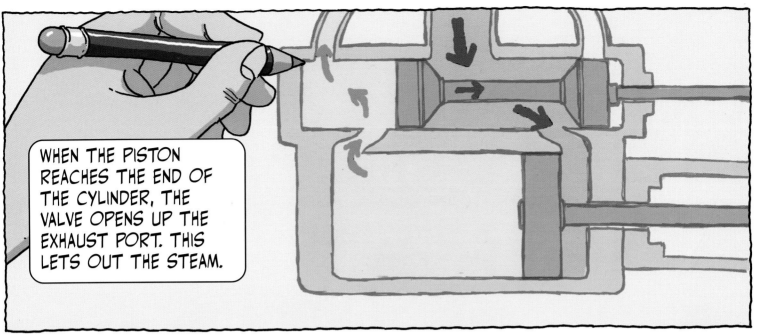

WHEN THE PISTON REACHES THE END OF THE CYLINDER, THE VALVE OPENS UP THE EXHAUST PORT. THIS LETS OUT THE STEAM.

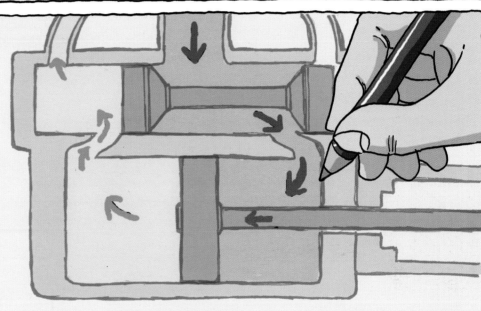

THE VALVE ALSO ALLOWS HIGH PRESSURE STEAM TO ENTER FROM THE RIGHT. THIS PUSHES THE PISTON TO THE OTHER END OF THE CYLINDER.

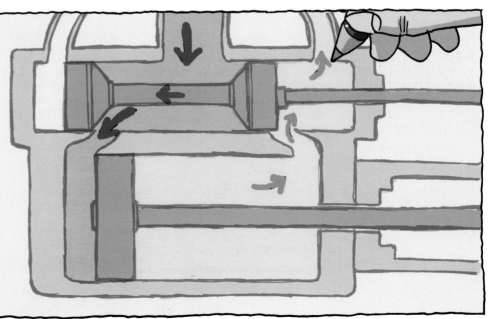

WHEN THE PISTON REACHES THE END OF THE CYLINDER, THE VALVE OPENS UP THE EXHAUST PORT ON THE OTHER SIDE TO ALLOW THE EXPANDED STEAM OUT. THE WHOLE PROCESS IS READY TO START AGAIN.

WHY DOESN'T THE TRAIN WORK, GRANDMA?

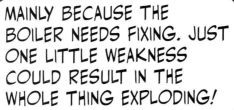

MAINLY BECAUSE THE BOILER NEEDS FIXING. JUST ONE LITTLE WEAKNESS COULD RESULT IN THE WHOLE THING EXPLODING!

EVEN WHEN THIS TRAIN WAS RUNNING IN THE FIRST HALF OF THE TWENTIETH CENTURY, IT WOULD NEED TO HAVE THE BOILER REPAIRED EVERY FIVE YEARS.

WE'VE NEARLY FINISHED, THOUGH.

WHAT ARE THOSE PIPES FOR?

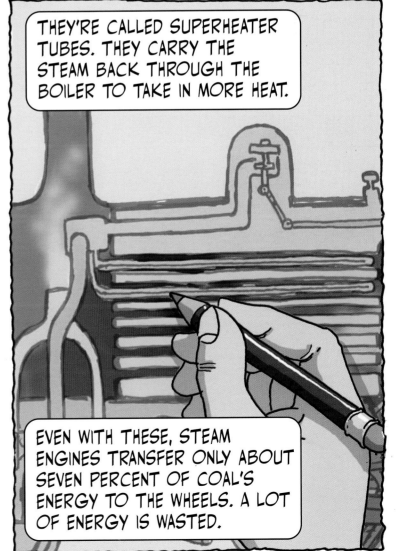

THEY'RE CALLED SUPERHEATER TUBES. THEY CARRY THE STEAM BACK THROUGH THE BOILER TO TAKE IN MORE HEAT.

EVEN WITH THESE, STEAM ENGINES TRANSFER ONLY ABOUT SEVEN PERCENT OF COAL'S ENERGY TO THE WHEELS. A LOT OF ENERGY IS WASTED.

WHAT IS THIS PIPE, HERE?

THAT'S WHERE THE SPENT STEAM FROM THE PISTONS' EXHAUST PORT COMES OUT.

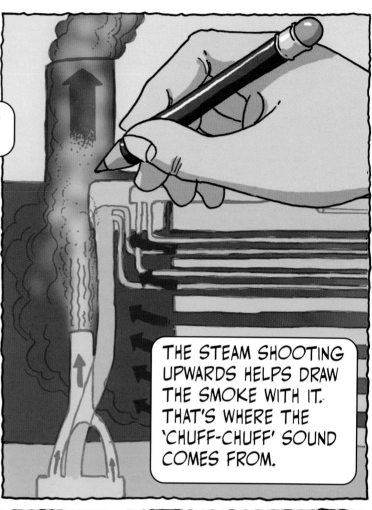

THE STEAM SHOOTING UPWARDS HELPS DRAW THE SMOKE WITH IT. THAT'S WHERE THE 'CHUFF-CHUFF' SOUND COMES FROM.

BY THE END OF THE WEEK, THE TANK ENGINE WAS FINISHED.

THE BOILER HAD BEEN COMPLETELY OVERHAULED.

THE PISTONS HAD BEEN CLEANED AND PUT BACK TOGETHER.

THE SMOKEBOX DOOR HAD BEEN FIXED BACK ON.

THE CHIMNEY HAD BEEN FITTED.

AND ALL THE RODS HAD BEEN OILED AND PUT BACK ON.

FINALLY, WE CLEANED THE WHOLE TRAIN OF RUST...

WHERE DOES RUST COME FROM?

IT'S A CHEMICAL REACTION CALLED **OXIDIZATION**, WHEN OXYGEN IN THE DAMP AIR REACTS WITH THE IRON.

AND REPAINTED IT.

PAINTING THE METAL HELPS PROTECT IT FROM RUSTING.

THE NEXT MORNING...

LOOK. THERE'S SMOKE COMING FROM THE CHIMNEY.

HI, KIDS. CLIMB UP ON TO THE FOOTPLATE. WE'RE BUILDING UP STEAM, READY FOR A TEST RUN.

SHOVEL SOME MORE COAL IN, PETER.

PEEEEEEEEEE----EEEP

THE SAFETY VALVE IS STUCK OPEN.

IF THE PRESSURE BUILDS UP TOO MUCH THIS VALVE OPENS UP TO LET OFF STEAM.

Valve

Steam

High pressure steam

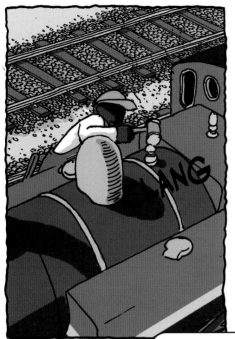

THAT'S SORTED IT OUT.

KEEP SHOVELLING THAT COAL, PETER.

LOOK. THE PRESSURE GAUGE SHOWS WE HAVE ENOUGH PRESSURE TO START.

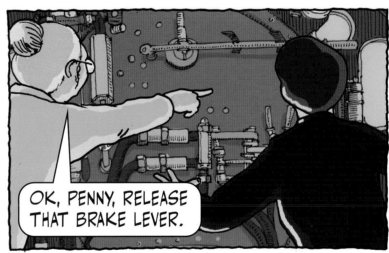

OK, PENNY, RELEASE THAT BRAKE LEVER.

PETER, PULL THE **THROTTLE LEVER,** THERE.

THAT OPENS THE THROTTLE VALVE IN THE STEAM DOME, WHICH LETS THE STEAM THROUGH TO THE PISTONS.

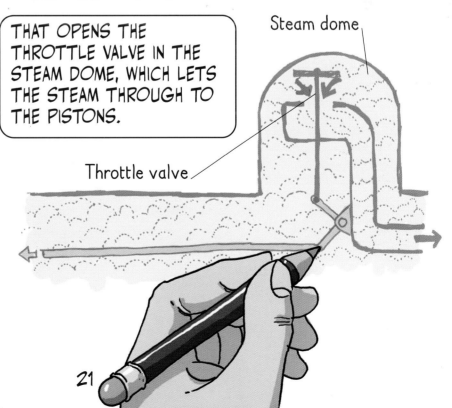

Steam dome

Throttle valve

WE'RE MOVING!

PULL THAT CORD TO BLOW THE WHISTLE.

CHUFF

THAT LETS STEAM RUSH THROUGH A WHISTLE, JUST LIKE ON OUR KETTLE.

CHUFF

CHUFF CHUFF CHUFF CHUFF

KEEP FEEDING THAT FIRE, PETER.

22

HALF AN HOUR LATER...

WE NEED TO STOP NOW AND HEAD BACK.

HOW DO WE TURN ROUND?

CRANK

WE DON'T NEED TO. WE JUST REVERSE THE WHEELS BY PULLING ON THAT LEVER.

THE ENGINE STARTED GOING BACKWARDS.

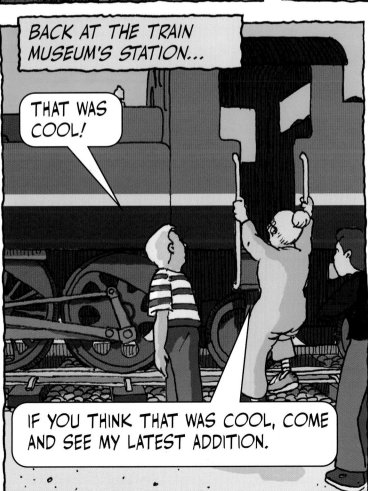

BACK AT THE TRAIN MUSEUM'S STATION...

THAT WAS COOL!

IF YOU THINK THAT WAS COOL, COME AND SEE MY LATEST ADDITION.

WOW! WHAT IS IT?

IT'S A FRENCH HIGH-SPEED ELECTRIC TRAIN, CALLED A TGV.

23

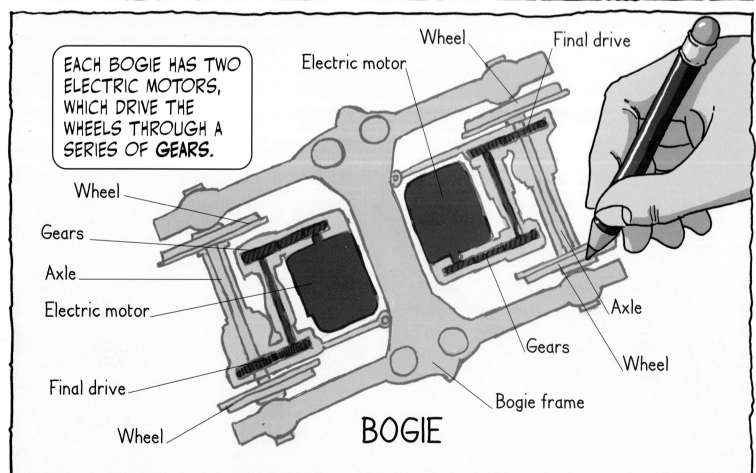

BOGIE

24

HOW DO ELECTRIC MOTORS WORK?

INSIDE AN ELECTRIC MOTOR ARE COILS OF WIRE WRAPPED AROUND A CENTRAL SPINDLE.

Coils of wire

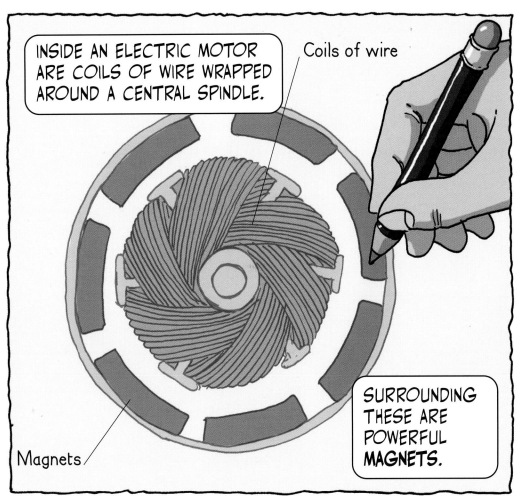

Magnets

SURROUNDING THESE ARE POWERFUL **MAGNETS.**

WHEN ELECTRICITY PASSES THROUGH THE COILS OF WIRE, THEY CREATE A MAGNETIC FIELD OPPOSITE TO THOSE OF THE MAGNETS.

Opposite poles attract. Similar poles **repel**.

THIS MAKES THE COILS OF WIRE **ROTATE,** WHICH CREATES A STRONG TURNING FORCE.

WHERE DOES THE TRAIN GET ITS ELECTRICITY FROM?

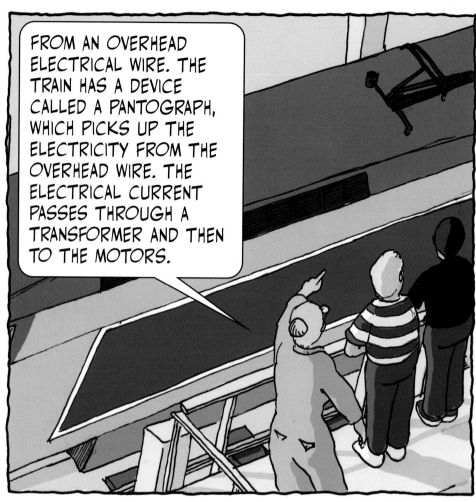

FROM AN OVERHEAD ELECTRICAL WIRE. THE TRAIN HAS A DEVICE CALLED A PANTOGRAPH, WHICH PICKS UP THE ELECTRICITY FROM THE OVERHEAD WIRE. THE ELECTRICAL CURRENT PASSES THROUGH A TRANSFORMER AND THEN TO THE MOTORS.

WHAT'S A TRANSFORMER?

ELECTRICITY IN THE OVERHEAD WIRE IS AT A VERY HIGH VOLTAGE. THE MOTORS USE A LOWER VOLTAGE. THE TRAIN HAS A TRANSFORMER TO CHANGE THE VOLTAGE SO THE MOTORS CAN USE IT. THIS DIAGRAM SHOWS HOW A TRANSFORMER WORKS.

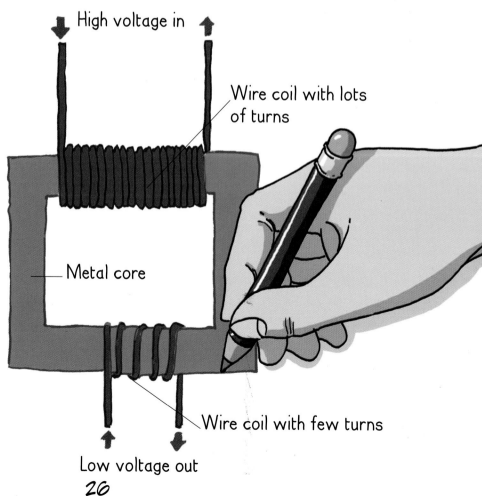

High voltage in

Wire coil with lots of turns

Metal core

Wire coil with few turns

Low voltage out

26

THIS IS A **REPLICA** OF THE FIRST EVER STEAM TRAIN. IT WAS BUILT BY TREVITHICK IN 1803.

THIS ONE HAS A DEVICE ON THE FRONT CALLED A COW CATCHER.

LOOK AT THIS PICTURE OF BIG BOY. THIS WAS THE BIGGEST STEAM TRAIN EVER BUILT.

28

THIS IS THE MALLARD, BUILT IN 1938, WHICH STILL HOLDS THE RECORD FOR THE FASTEST STEAM TRAIN AT TWO HUNDRED AND TWO KILOMETRES PER HOUR.

HERE'S A PICTURE OF THE FASTEST ELECTRIC TRAIN. IT'S A JAPANESE BULLET TRAIN. IT'S GOT AIR BRAKES THAT LOOK LIKE EARS.

HERE'S A PICTURE OF A TRAIN THAT HOVERS ON MAGNETS! IT'S CALLED A MAGLEV TRAIN.

FINALLY IT WAS TIME TO GO. GRANDMA DROPPED PETER AND PENNY AT THE TRAIN STATION.

THANKS FOR HELPING ME OUT, KIDS. I'LL LET YOU KNOW WHEN THE TGV IS READY.

LOOK! IT'S THE SAME TRAIN AS GRANDMA'S!

29

Parts of a steam train

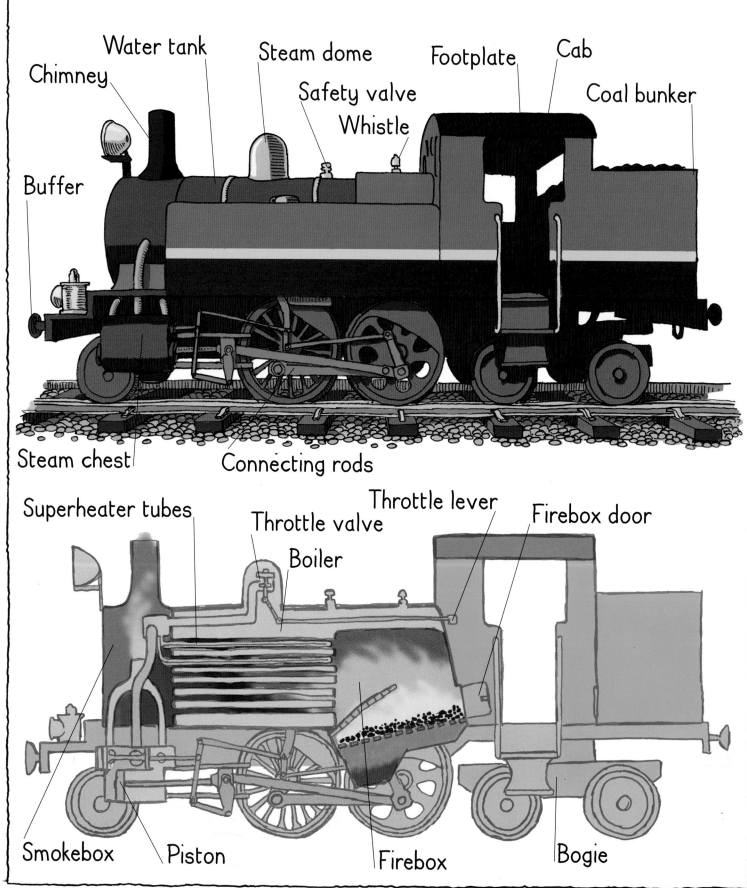

Chimney

Water tank

Steam dome

Footplate

Cab

Safety valve

Whistle

Coal bunker

Buffer

Steam chest

Connecting rods

Superheater tubes

Throttle valve

Throttle lever

Firebox door

Boiler

Smokebox

Piston

Firebox

Bogie

Glossary

BOGIE
FRAME WITH FOUR WHEELS THAT
SUPPORTS THE TRAIN

BOILER
METAL CONTAINER HOLDING WATER THAT
IS TURNED INTO STEAM

COAL BUNKER
PLACE WHERE THE COAL IS STORED

COMPUTER
AN ELECTRONIC DEVICE THAT CAN BE
PROGRAMMED TO CONTROL THE VARIOUS
WORKINGS OF A MACHINE.

CONNECTING RODS
THE METAL RODS ATTACHED TO THE
PISTONS AND THE WHEELS, WHICH TURN
THE WHEELS

CYLINDER
THE METAL SLEEVE INSIDE WHICH A
PISTON MOVES

EXHAUST PORT
THE HOLES IN THE STEAM CHEST
THROUGH WHICH THE EXPANDED
STEAM EXITS

FIREBOX
THE PLACE, INSIDE A STEAM TRAIN, WHERE
THE COAL IS BURNT

GEARS
A SET OF WHEELS THAT TRANSFER
POWER. THE WHEELS HAVE TEETH ON
THEIR RIM, WHICH ALLOWS THEM TO
GRIP EACH OTHER.

HIGH PRESSURE STEAM
STEAM THAT IS VERY HOT AND HAS NOT
BEEN ALLOWED TO EXPAND

MAGNET
A PIECE OF METAL, USUALLY IRON, WHICH
HAS A MAGNETIC FIELD WITH NORTH AND
SOUTH POLES

OXIDIZATION
THE PROCESS OF RUSTING, WHEN A
METAL, SUCH AS IRON, COMBINES WITH
OXYGEN IN A DAMP ATMOSPHERE

PISTON
A SOLID CYLINDER THAT MOVES TO AND
FRO INSIDE ANOTHER, HOLLOW CYLINDER

REPEL
TO FORCE AWAY

REPLICA
A COPY

ROTATE
TURN

RUST
THE RESULT OF OXYDIZATION

THROTTLE LEVER
THE CONTROL, WHICH MAKES THE TRAIN
GO FASTER OR SLOWER

VALVE
A DEVICE THAT OPENS AND CLOSES,
ALLOWING A GAS OR LIQUID THROUGH AN
OPENING – USUALLY ONLY ONE WAY

Index

Motorcycles

an illustrated history

Erwin Tragatsch

Motorcycles

an illustrated history

Galley Press

Galley Press – an imprint owned by W.H.Smith
& Son Ltd.
Trading as WHS Distributors, St Johns House,
East Street, Leicester LE1 6NE.

This book was designed and produced by
Quarto Publishing Limited, 32 Kingly Court,
London W1.

Phototypeset in England by Filmtype Services
Limited, Scarborough
Colour separation by Sakai Lithocolour
Company Limited, Hong Kong
Printed by Leefung-Asco Printers Limited,
Hong Kong

BN 0 86136 018 4

CONTENTS

Triumphant moment . . . the author worked for the British firm in the 1950s

The word *motorcycle* was first used to describe a bicycle with an internal combustion engine in 1893; although the first bicycle with an engine had appeared some 20 years earlier, it was powered by steam, and it was not until the advent of the petrol engine that a successful motorcycle was made. The idea spread rapidly, motorcycles soon became widely available in Europe and America, and a new and popular means of transport had arrived.

Motorcycles, An Illustrated History describes the wordwide development of the motorcycle from those pioneering days to the advanced technology of the 1970s. The opening chapter deals with the development of the industry from the early machines produced by Hildebrand and Wolfmüller to the post-Second World War success story of Japanese technology. The history of the motorcycle is then traced from the pioneer years of the 1890s, through the machines developed during the First World War and the post-war boom during the 1920s to the designs which appeared during the Second World War. There is a chapter on the great designers, and the book concludes with details of the classics superbly illustrated in full colour: here are the Henderson and the Harley-Davidson, the Scott and the Brough Superior, the Ducati Desmo and the Yamaha twins – the all-time classic machines through the decades.

THE STORY OF AN INDUSTRY

THE HISTORY of the motorcycle also offers a short course in design philosophy and industrial economics, with some politics thrown in.

Great pioneers like Hildebrand and Wolfmüller were clever inventors, but their design went into production without any development work. The result was that the factory went broke in a very few years. The same fate befell Colonel H. C. L. Holden's 'moto-bicycle', which had four horizontal watercooled cylinders directly driving the rear wheel. This, too, was an ingenious design, but was already obsolete before it would have gone into quantity production in 1900. In France, the Russian-born Werner brothers, Michael and Eugene, built a motorcycle to a design using De Dion proprietary engines from 52 to 70mm bore and always a 70mm stroke. The 70/70 model built in 1899 had 2·25 hp (269cc). These were smaller and lighter engines than had been used before. After 1902, they used strengthened bicycle frames, mounting the engine above the pedalling gear, and this machine became the ancestor of motorcycles as we know them today.

A practical basic design had been established, but the story of the motorcycle continued to be a story of designers and technicians who sometimes had no commercial sense. There were also designs which worked briefly but which look strange to modern eyes: the German Megola, designed by Fritz Cockerell, was clutchless and gearless, and had to be started by being pushed. It would be hope-lessly impractical, and even dangerous, in modern traffic, but more than 2000 of them were sold in the 1920s.

The founders of the great motorcycle factories had to be visionary men of great technical ability and with no small amount of idealism. The profit margin in this developing competitive business was usually lower than that in other industries. It often happened that when the founder died or retired, the factory went into decline, being managed by industrialists rather than motorcycle men: a good example of this was the Indian factory at Springfield, Massachusetts. In 1912, Indian was one of the largest motorcycle factories in the world, employing about 3,000 people on three shifts. When founder George M. Hendee retired in the mid-1920s, the factory began a long, slow decline. When it was finally bought in 1959 by Associated Motor Cycles Ltd., of London, the only thing left was the Indian name on motorcycles produced for the American market.

Designers were often people who wanted to sell their designs to others, and get on with something new. They were often less interested in the continuous development of a machine once it was in production. So it was that William Henderson created his big four-cylinder aircooled Henderson, sold it and went on to design the not dissimilar Ace. After Henderson's death in an accident in 1922, it was Arthur Lemon who continued development work on the Henderson for Ignaz Schwinn's Chicago-based bicycle company. On the other hand, sometimes a good design has been develop-ed but basically unchanged for many years because of its intrinsic excellence: the best example of this is the famous BMW twin. Since the machine was first shown in Paris in 1923, BMW has never built a twin which was not horizontally opposed, mounted transversely in the frame and which did not drive a shaft rather than a chain. The original designer was Max Friz.

The motorcycle industry, like any other, is also subject to factors outside its control. A great many factories went under during the Great Depression of the 1930s, to say nothing of the German hyper-inflation of 1923. After each of the two world wars, motorcycles were in such short supply that small companies sprang up in every country, doing well for a short time with designs which in many cases were essentially undistinguished. When Hitler gobbled up Central Europe in the late 1930s, some small producers of motorcycles disappeared because they could not be fitted into the Nazis' industrial plans.

By contrast, the Italian motorcycle industry has broken nearly every rule in the book: before the Second World War, the Italians built good machines, but did not try very hard to export them; since the war, while the Italian economy may have experienced its vicissitudes, a surprising number of relatively small producers, as well as a few big ones, have managed to stay in business. They have also continued to uphold the traditional Italian reputation for good design. There has been no lack of great designers in the Italian industry: Carlo Guzzi's designs in developed form

The 1920s was the boom period for the small manufacturer, though producers like BMW (left, top) had already adopted a methodical approach. Half a century later, the masters of the production line are the Japanese, with Kawasaki (bottom picture) among the leaders.

became the famous Albatross racers. Angelo Parodi, Giulo Carcano and Lino Tonti also helped to design the Moto Guzzi machines; in the mid-1950s, Carcano was designing four-cylinder and V-8 double-ohc racing machines. In the late 1950s, very fine Bianchi double-ohc vertical twins were designed by Tonti, who then went on to create transverse-mounted V-twins with shaft drive for Moto Guzzi. The six Benelli brothers and many others have contributed to the excellence of Italian machines; yet today, even the Italian industry is falling victim to the post-war trend towards industrial conglomeration.

The saddest story of all is the decline of the British motorcycle industry, for decades the world's leader. The incompetence of management, and of various governments, has seen the British motorcycle industry lose its leadership by default. For one thing, it is not possible to stay in the motorcycle business on any sizable scale unless a wide range of models is offered. In the face of Japanese competition, British factories gave up the mass-production of small machines; for some years thereafter, British superbikes were still very popular, but it was no longer economically feasible to build them.

The Japanese deserve their success, there can be no doubt about that. The Honda factory has stayed on top because it has been ready to re-invest its profits in up-to-date plant and equipment, and because Soichiro Honda does not need weeks or months of consultation with banks, Boards of Directors and numerous unions before making a decision. The character of designing has also changed: if Mike Mizumachi is responsible for the

brilliant success of the Kawasaki factory, it is also true that he has not done it single-handedly, but is the head of a brilliant team of younger men who will no doubt become famous in their own right. Times have changed. The motorcycle business is no different from any other; only people who can change with the times can stay on top.

The motorcycle factories which survived the Great Depression were those which were large and strong, and which already had networks of dealers and customers dependent on a good name for service, spare parts and so forth. The day of the committed idealist who could start his own factory on a shoe-string was past. Designers became less freelance geniuses and more valued employees of established manufacturers. Even before the Second World War, the process of combination began in which, for example, Matchless swallowed AJS to become Associated Motor Cycles which in turn took over Francis Barnett, James, Norton – and even the American Indian factory after WWII.

In the post-war years this process accelerated, until it actually became uneconomic to build motorcycles in countries with high per-capita incomes. In the 1920s, there were perhaps fifteen different companies building very good machines in the USA; eventually only Harley-Davidson was left. Even Harley had to buy the Italian Aermacchi works in order to produce comparatively small machines at competitive prices. Small countries such as The Netherlands, Belgium, Denmark and Switzerland once had notable indigenous producers; today motorcycle production in these countries is virtually nil. Nations such as Italy and Spain, which have the

design and engineering skill but which are relatively undeveloped, have thriving motorcycle industries because they are economically competitive.

The special cases are Socialist countries, such as Czechoslovakia and East Germany. Whatever else one might say about nationalized industry, these countries produce their own two-wheeled transport and they have no unemployment to speak of. Another special case is Britain, the world's leader for decades; during the 1950s, British imports spelled the end of much American competition in the industry. Yet today Britain's industry is almost finished. It is perhaps not too much to say that part of Britain's problem is that it can't decide what kind of economics it wants; certainly the measures it has taken in the motorcycle industry are half-measures. Britain has the skills, and with the fall of the Pound it should be economically competitive; one can only hope that it will have a Renaissance of spirit.

The overwhelming factor in the post-war motorcycle industry has been Japan. In 1970, Britain built about 64,500 machines; Germany built about 70,000, and Japan built nearly three million. The fact that Japan has beaten the Western countries at their own game, and in a very short time, is a tribute to her industry and her single-mindedness, but she has also brought Western-style problems upon herself. In the electronics industry, even the Japanese are farming out work to places like Taiwan. What the world's industry will look like when there are no poor people left to exploit is anybody's guess: at any rate, motorcycles as transport and for racing are as popular today as they have ever been.

MOTORCYCLE PRODUCTION IN MAIN MANUFACTURING NATIONS

Country:	1969	1970	1971	1972	1973	1974	1975
Austria	4,278	7,044	7,643	11,768	12,253	14,244	10,746
Britain	71,010	64,521	86,650	48,832	48,439	40,000	
Czechoslovakia				270,000			118,566
France	3,375	4,292	6,508	6,627	8,686	9,038	8,513
Germany	52,568	70,123	66,462	69,099	84,357	66,901	74,660
Italy	580,000	560,000	617,000	682,500	694,500	795,500	833,000
Japan	2,576,873	2,947,672	3,400,502	3,565,246	3,767,327	4,509,420	3,802,547
Spain	32,514	30,437	36,661	49,465	54,176	59,747	58,351

THE PIONEER YEARS

IT IS IMPOSSIBLE to bestow on any individual the credit for having 'invented' the motorcycle. There was much preliminary development to be accomplished before any kind of motor vehicle could be practical.

In 1876, Nikolaus August Otto built a four-stroke internal combustion engine. Dugald Clerk, in 1877-78, developed a two-stroke compression machine with a charging pump. In 1883, Gottlieb Daimler and Wilhelm Maybach invented surface ignition, which made possible a fast-running lightweight engine. Otto invented a low-tension make-and-break (coil) ignition in 1884, and the next year Daimler and Maybach built a two-wheeled vehicle with a wooden frame and belt drive. Finally, in 1894 Heinrich Hildebrand and Alois Wolfmüller designed the first commercially-built two-wheeler to be called a motorcycle.

In 1895 there were French three-wheelers using the De Dion engines, such as the Gladiator, and in England the Beeston. The year 1896 saw the quantity manufacture of these engines, and in 1897 the Werner machine appeared in Paris with the engine above the front wheel. Soon, the Werners also had a factory in London. The Coventry Motor Company was building machines in the city of the same name, in the industrial Midlands of England. In the same city, Humber and Beeston were in production. In the same year, Italy's Edoardo Bianchi commenced production. In 1898, the factory of Georges Bouton and Count De Dion began production of a three-wheeler, using their own 239cc engine.

De Dion engines were extremely successful. By 1899, they had overtaken the Hildebrand and Wolfmüller design; in that year, Laurin and Klement began motorcycle production in what was then the Austro-Hungarian Empire, using the 239cc De Dion engine until they developed their own. Engines were also being made by Sarolea in Belgium, and a clever Frenchman called André Boudeville began manufacture of high-tension magnetos in Paris. 1899 also saw the first 211cc Minerva engine, the first engine-assisted Raleigh bicycles, the first Matchless motorcycles

Early days in France and Germany . . . Above: the first Daimler and Maybach two-wheeler (left) and the 1894 Hildebrand & Wolfmüller. Bottom: the Parisian Werner Motocyclette, and the De Dion-Bouton three-wheeler. T. Tessier broke a speed record on an English BAT (right) in 1903.

THOSE MAGNIFICENT MEN ON THEIR CYCLING MACHINES

A steam engine, fired by petrol, powered this von Sauerbronn-Davis velocipede, 1883

The 1887 Millet prototype had a radial engine similar to those later used in aircraft

Propellor power . . . a chitty, chitty, bang bike by Anzani had its test flight in 1906

Look, no pedals! An ordinary bicycle gets a shove from an auxiliary engine . . . Italy, 1893

'Luxurious, high-powered, all-weather car-ette' . . . twin engined Quadrant, made in Britain, 1905

Where to put the engine? Above the front wheel, perhaps? That (1) was Werner's solution, in 1899. Enfield placed the engine in the same place, but to drive the rear wheel

Strange layouts abounded at the turn of the century . . . Singer positioned the engine in the hub of the front wheel (2). Further variations came from British Excelsior (3), Phelon and Moore (4), Hildebrand and Wolfmüller (5), Beeston (6), Ormonde (7), Singer again (8) and Humber (9).

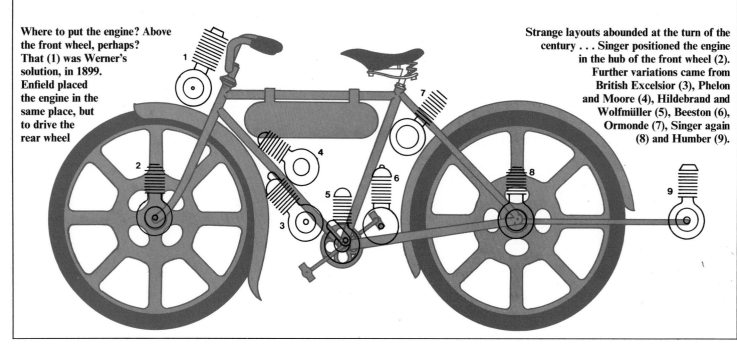

and the first motorcycle races: at the Friedenauer Cycle Track in Germany and the Exelberg in Austria.

The first year of the new century brought the introduction of the Perks & Birch (later Singer) motor wheel, Joah Phelon's first P&M motorcycle, the first Excelsiors built by Bayliss-Thomas, and in America, the Orient motorcycle designed by Charles H. Metz. In 1901, Swedish-American Oscar Hedström built the first Indian motorcycle, and the Werners experimented with vertical engines mounted in the centre of the frame. Puch and NSU built their first motorcycles, the latter using the Swiss Zedel engine. In England, Yorkshire's Alfred Angas Scott began the development of his unorthodox two-stroke engines, which are still famous today. Also in 1901, Orient became the first American company to export a machine to Europe. Emil Hafelfinger, also an American, created the first two-speed gear, and Condor, a Swiss factory, began producing motorized bicycles.

Also in Switzerland, the Dufaux brothers began producing bicycle attachment engines, calling their product Motosacoche (engine in the pocket). The same factory later produced the MAG engine, playing the same part on the Continent as JAP (J. A. Prestwich & Co. Ltd.) in England, who began producing proprietary engines in 1902. (The Swiss factory always made complete machines as well, but the London factory after 1908 made engines only.) The year also saw the manufacture of ohv engines by the French Clément works, Strickland's design of vertical twins, and Ariel's first motorcycles, built in Birmingham with Belgian Kerry engines. Wicker sidecars were being made by Mills & Fulford in Coventry.

The aircooled four-cylinder FN, with shaft drive, came into quantity production in 1903. Another four was built by Charles Binks, and Buchet in France was supplying a vertical twin with no less than 4245cc capacity. Shaft-driven singles were built by FN and by William Starley. White & Poppe began building 3 hp single-cylinder proprietary engines. America saw the first Harley-Davidson motorcycle, made in Milwaukee, Wisconsin. Triumph, in Britain, began making their own engines; with the help of Bettmann and Schulte, the two Germans who had come to Coventry to found Triumph, the German

company of the same name began to build motorcycles in Nuremberg. The British BAT machine had a spring frame; the factory at Penge was owned by the Tessier family. It was widely thought that BAT stood for 'best after test', but the designer's name was Batson.

In France the Bichrone two-stroke was installed in Griffon frames. In 1904 the International Coupé Race in France became the first international motorcycle event. Demester of France won it riding a Griffon; number two was Toman riding a Laurin & Klement. Automatic inlet valves became common on engines and Peugeot of France now used Truffault's swinging arm forks. Dürkopp and Laurin & Klement built four-in-line engines. While England had 21,521 machines registered, only 776 were exported. Hercules and Victoria of Germany entered the market, and a Peugeot rider reached 76·5 mph on a machine weighing 110 pounds.

The following year, 1905, saw the introduction in England of quantity production of Scott's, not yet at the famous works in Shipley, Yorkshire, but at the Jowett works in nearby Bradford. Another new make was the Fairy, with a horizontally opposed twin designed by J. Barter. This was the forerunner of the Douglas. There were more vertical twins, too; the Belgian Bercley designed by Gustave Kindermann and Eugene Werner's own Werner, built in Paris. Both the Werner brothers, great pioneers of motorcycling, died the same year.

There was a switch to magneto ignition by most factories in 1906. In that year the

The start of the first T.T. race in 1908 (inset, far left), and the twin-cylinder class winner Harry Reed astride his D.O.T. Big picture: the circuit's notorious Devil's Elbow. Bottom: winner of the 1905 International Coupe, Václav Vondrich, on a CCR.

British firm of JAP built the first ohv V-twin engines. A JAP engine powered the first three-cylinder Dennell, from Yorkshire. The same county produced the P&M, which had a two-speed gear, with clutch. The year 1906 also saw the first Druid spring forks. The year before, Václav Vondřich, riding a Laurin & Klement V-twin, had won the Coupé International, but in 1906 it was the Austrian Edward Nikodem, on a Puch.

After this race, British riders complained about the bad organisation, and mainly about the interpretation of the rules by certain Continental teams. After their return they decided to start their own event, and the result was the first Tourist Trophy race in the Isle of Man. This was in 1907, the same year that a trade slump caused the disappearance of some motorcycle producers. Glenn Curtis, an American manufacturer of aircraft engines, allegedly reached an unofficial 130 mph using a modified transverse-mounted V-8. Douglas had started quantity production of their machines with the Barter-designed flat-twin engine, and Eysink in Holland introduced their own vertical twins. 1908 saw the opening of Brooklands, the famous racetrack at Weybridge, south of London. It also saw the first Italian entrant in the TT race, riding an English Rex. A new design by the Dufaux brothers had a seven-cylinder rotary engine built into the rear wheel. This was the first and last seven ever built.

Triumphs in England got hub clutches in their rear wheels in 1909, a very good design by Maurice Schulte. That year also saw the P. G. Tacchi-designed Wilkinson TAC (Touring Auto Cycle, with a steering wheel) which soon became the TMC (Touring Motor Cycle, with handlebars). Both had aircooled (or optionally watercooled) four-in-line engines, and both were built by the Wilkinson Sword Company, later famous for razor blades. The Stevens brothers began manufacture of complete motorcycles called AJS. Renouf's James design was interesting, with its chassis-type frame and a spring seat pillar. Giuseppe Gilera's was a new make. At Brooklands, an NLG (North London Garages) reached 90 mph with an ohv V-twin of 2713cc built by JAP. The rider was W. E. Cook. F. A. McNab broke the one-hour record riding a Trump, which also had a JAP engine. McNab was one of the owners of the Trump factory.

A motorcycle boom started in 1910, but didn't help the new Renouf-designed James, a horizontally-opposed two-stroke twin with overheating problems. Britain had exported £24,202 worth of motorcycles in 1909, and more than doubled it in 1910 to £53,661. The boom in the USA resulted in 86,414 registrations. In Britain, Zenith's Fred Barnes designed the famous Gradua gear and a spring frame.

In 1911 the American Indian machines scored a 1-2-3 victory in the Senior TT, the biggest shock for the British industry

The T.T. attracted competitors from many countries. This Italian team is gathered for the 1926 Junior T.T.; Edoardo Bianchi is third from left. The Indian 'Hendee Special' of 1914 (bottom) was the first motorcycle with an electric self-starter.

until the Japanese invasion of the 1960s. The Indians were ridden by O. C. Godfrey, C. B. Franklin and A. J. Moorhouse. Rudge (Rudge Whitworth) came onto the scene that year with a 499cc single which had overhead-inlet and side-exhaust valves and which afterwards got the well-known Multi gear. Britain's motorcycle exports rose to the value of £120,289 and Charlie Collier — one of the three brothers of Matchless fame — broke the official world record with 91·37 mph. In France, Meuriot rode a Rene-Gillet at the Gomez-le-Chatel hill climb. The machine had a cross-shaped four-cylinder 20 hp engine which was really a radial. John Wooler built his first machine: a 346cc two-stroke with a horizontal cylinder and an additional pumping piston in the crankcase. (The same John Wooler was designing four-cylinder machines 40 years later, after the Second World War.) 1911 was also a busy year in America, with Bill Henderson creating his aircooled four-in-line, Pope building 498cc singles and 996cc ohv V-twins, and Jack Prince building a famous racetrack at Los Angeles.

Sunbeam machines entered the market in 1912. Designed by J. E. Greenwood and built at Wolverhampton in the West Midlands of England, they were of outstanding design and quality, among the finest machines ever built. Also from Wolverhampton came the Villiers proprietary engines, which in those far-off days were four-strokes, not the two-strokes we knew so well later. During this period, the Indian factory was a busy, thriving place, and the Italian Bianchi factory was the same. In 1912, founder Edoardo Bianchi

at the age of 45 was made a *Cavaliere del Lavoro*. Alas, Sunbeam, Indian and Bianchi are all gone today.

C. B. Redrup designed his first three-cylinder radial engine in 1912; Rex in Coventry and others built two-speed countershafts in front of the engines; ASL, a spring factory, built motorcycles with spring frames. In races, Charlie and Harry Collier of Matchless fame used new six-speed gearboxes. At Brooklands, they got more American competition in the form of H. A. Shaw on a 7 hp Thor and J. E. Hogge on a 4 hp Indian. A boost for two-strokes came in the Isle of Man, when Frank Applebee won the Senior TT on a 3·5 hp Scott with an average speed of 48·70 mph, and the fastest lap with 49·44 mph. G. E.

Stanley's hour record at Brooklands stood until 1920.

The Americans went on and on. Harley-Davidsons got chain drive to replace the belt drive; Indian supplied some models with full electrical equipment, a rarity in those days. In 1913 Andrew Strand designed with John McNeill the first commercially-built 996cc ohc V-twin, the Cyclone, and many were sold to private sportsmen in the USA.

Technically, the most outstanding motorcycle of 1913 was the 494cc vertical twin Peugeot racing machine, designed by Antoinescu, but based on the Peugeot racing car engine design of 1912. This double-ohc engine was re-designed many times and was still winning races in 1927; it was never sold to private entrants. Triumph in England experimented with a vertical twin, and Humber with a three-cylinder model, but they never went into quantity production. A new English sporting event, the International Sixdays Trial, was introduced and is still with us. Russia was in the news when a rider from that country participated in the Senior TT; his name was Kremleff. He rode a Rudge and retired after a crash.

Britain had by this time 179,926 registered motorcycles, the Americans produced 70,000 machines in 1913 and Carl Goudy, riding an American Schwinn-built Excelsior, won the 100 mile race at Columbus. A new Indian was the 2·25 hp two-stroke 211cc machine.

THE FIRST WORLD WAR

As THE 1914 WAR BROKE OUT in Europe, the Chicago-based Schwinn-owned Excelsior Company moved to new works at 3700 Cortland Street. Glen Boyd won on an Indian the first race at Dodge City. In Britain. Cyril Pullin on a Rudge and Eric Williams on an sv AJS won the last pre-first-war Senior and Junior TT races. Jack Emerson took an ABC with a Bradshaw-designed 496cc flat-twin engine to Brooklands and got a speed of 80·47 mph. Despite the world political situation, the British motorcycle industry exported 20,877 motorcycles. Puch, the Austrian factory, built machines with horizontally opposed cylinders. Burman in England, famous for gears and gearboxes, entered the manufacture of proprietary engines, but the war prevented their mass production.

Motorcycles played an important part in the war. The British used mainly Triumph, Douglas, P&M, Clyno and Sunbeams: the Germans NSU and Wanderer machines; the French René Gillets, the Austrians Puchs and the Italians Bianchis and a variety of other makes. Britain supplied machines to the Czar of Russia, including Rovers and Premiers. A cargo of 250 Premier machines was sunk in the North Sea on its way to Russia.

Premier built in 1915 the prototype of a new 322cc two-stroke vertical twin. For two years they developed it, but never began quantity production. It was in fact the last Premier ever made in Coventry; soon after the war, the factory was bought by Singer. Also new was a 90-degree V-twin, made by Phelon & Moore at Cleckheaton, in Yorkshire, the works which supplied many singles to the British Air Force during the war. Like the Premier, it

During the First World War, the American Forces ordered 70,000 Harleys, some rigged as armed outfits (above). Britain had a Clyno-Vickers machine-gun outfit (below).

was never built in quantities. The same applied to a new watercooled 746cc flat-twin made by Humber. Britain registered 147,904 motorcycles and exported 10,979.

America was still having big races. Otto Walker, riding a Harley-Davidson with a 996cc V-twin won at Dodge City; watching was Bill Ottoway, who had just created a new 8-valve ohv V-twin for racing on America's long tracks. He was at that time chief designer and head of the racing department at the famous Milwaukee factory. On this 8-valve Harley-Davidson

Historic border-crossing (left) by Harley-Davidson on Armistice Day, 1918. British dispatch-riders used machines by Phelan and Moore, Douglas, BSA, Triumph and others.

The first Yank and Harley to enter Germany 11/17/18

German dispatch-rider (below, left), in Düsseldorf. German Triumph motorcycles were used by the Kaiser's Forces, along with Neckarsulm (NSU) and Ardie machines. Below, right: British rider photographed in 1917 during the German East Africa campaign.

Jack Janke was the winner at Dodge City in 1916. In the same year, William Hendee —the founder of Indian at Springfield— sold most of his shares in the factory; Roy Artley, riding a four-cylinder Henderson, broke the Los Angeles to San Francisco record with 10 hours and 4 minutes and Britain's number of motorcycles stood, despite the war, at 153,000.

Motorcycle prices increased during the war; even in the USA one had to pay the equivalent of £170 for a 269cc two-stroke Cleveland. That was in 1917, when Indian built the first 996cc Powerplus V-twins, the 15 hp Thor V-twin got a reverse gear, Excelsior in Chicago bought the Henderson design and Harley-Davidson got a big Army order for their machines. In 1918, nearly all factories in the world worked for the war. Some prepared for peace; others were anxious because when the war was over they would lose valuable government contracts.

THE 1920s...THE GOLDEN AGE

THE FIRST YEAR OF PEACE saw much activity in the motorcycle industry. There was such a demand for machines that many factories switched over to the assembly or manufacture of motorcycles, without having the necessary experience or suitable equipment. Second-class machines, and even really bad ones, found customers, until the market was quite satisfied and buyers of motorcycles could tell good designs from bad ones. It was a technically interesting, but commercially unstable period. There were many producers which arrived from nowhere and soon disappeared, leaving behind unhappy customers and problems.

The year 1919 saw the introduction of a good two-stroke single, the 497cc Dunelt with the double-diameter piston, which created a certain amount of forced induction. In the USA appeared the first Bill Henderson-designed four-in-line ACE, which eventually became in 1927 the first Indian four. In Germany a new make, DKW, became famous for good two-strokes. The first one was designed by the very experienced Hugo Ruppe, who was also the creator of Bekamo two-strokes, which had wooden frames and a pumping piston in the crankcase for forced induction. Bekamos were to win many races in the early 1920s. Another new creation was the Bradshaw-designed 398cc ABC with the transverse-mounted flat-twin ohv engine, produced by the Sopwith Engineering Co. It was a modern conception, but was not fully developed when it was put on the market. Sunbeam became part of the Nobel (ICI) group.

In Italy, the 346cc Garelli with the double-piston two-stroke single-cylinder engine was another make which soon after the war gained popularity and successes in sporting events. Adalberto Garelli created this unorthodox design. A short-lived scooter boom swamped England. Alfred Angus Scott had sold his interests in the now Shipley-based Scott Motorcycle Company. The new make Francis Barnett bought the Bayliss-Thomas works at Coventry, after Bayliss-Thomas — manufacturers of English Excelsior motorcycles — had moved to Birmingham. The other Excelsior factory — owned by Ignaz Schwinn at Chicago — built new John McNeill-designed motorcycles with ohc racing engines (498cc and 996cc) for the works team, while Charles Franklin crea-

ted the famous 596cc sv V-twin Scout for Indian, one of the finest machines ever made in the USA. Franklin, an Irishman, had been one of the winners in the 1911 Senior TT.

A very interesting machine, the German Mars, was designed in 1920 by Franzenberg. It had a frame made from pressed steel plates which were welded and rivetted together.

The Mars' power unit was the only motorcycle engine ever built by the famous Maybach car and aero-engine works at Friedrichshafen. It had two horizontally-opposed cylinders, a capacity of 956cc and side valves. Starting was by a crank. This design was produced for nearly ten years in slightly developed form. And there was a motorcycle boom in nearly all countries; Britain had 280,000 registered machines, produced by nearly 200 different assemblers and manufacturers. A new design was a 248cc V-twin made by Diamond, but it never went into quantity production. The first official world speed record for motorcycles was established on April 14, 1920 by Ernie Walker at Daytona on a 994cc V-twin Indian with more than 101 mph. Racing in America was again in full swing and the leading factories such as

Indian, Harley-Davidson, Excelsior (including Henderson) and Reading-Standard competed in most events. Dodge City was won by Jim Davis on a Harley-Davidson, where there was a new flat-twin of 584cc with side-valves designed by Bill Ottoway.

Many new makes and models appeared in 1921. It was the year of the first Carlo Guzzi-designed 497cc Moto-Guzzi, with a horizontal single-cylinder ioe engine, and the first George Brough-designed 974cc Brough-Superior V-twin with a JAP engine. At Munich, the first Megola — the Fritz Cockerell-designed machine with a 5-cylinder radial engine of 640cc built directly into the front wheel — appeared on the scene. It had neither clutch nor gearbox. Around 2000 were built when after four years the factory closed down. It was also 1921 when Hugo Ruppe, who had created the first DKW, began manufacture of his own 129cc Bekamos. The same year, Sun in England used 269cc and afterwards 247cc Vitesse engines, two-strokes with a rotary valve on the induction side. Harry Ricardo, later Sir Harry Ricardo, was busy at Triumph in Coventry, developing his excellent 498cc ohv four-valve single-cylinder 'Riccy' model. Barr & Stroud of Glasgow began manufacture of 347cc sleeve-valve proprietary engines. Scotts got saddle-tanks. Scooters began to disappear, but motorcycles sold like hot cakes, despite the very high prices. Some examples: 247cc Levis two-stroke, £65; 799cc V-twin AJS with sidecar, £210; 748cc four-cylinder FN with shaft drive, £160; 490cc Norton with sv engine, £132.

Belgium had its first Grand Prix motorcycle race in 1921 and Ernst Neumann-Neander, the well-known German designer, created a prototype with an Adler-built 123cc engine. Italy had a TT race in 1921 at the Circuito del Lario and Amedeo Ruggeri — in the 1930s a Maserati racing-car driver — won it on a 998cc Harley-Davidson. The year's registration figure in the UK: 373,200; in the USA: 154,000. New in 1921 also was a 596cc V-twin Bianchi from Italy and a similar 494cc version made by Galloni; Benelli entered the market with a 98cc two-stroke. The V-twin 477cc Borgo racing machine had 8 valves and ohc, as well as a partly oil-cooled unit-design engine.

The many flat-twins built in 1921 mainly in Britain and Italy included the Fongri,

The post-war years saw a short-lived craze for the scooter (left). The unorthodox 5-cylinder Megola was raced by Toni Bauhofer and reached speeds up to 140 km/h.

Maxima, SAR, Raleigh, Humber, Wooler, Zenith, Dalton, Slaney, Brough, Douglas, Williamson, ABC and also the American Harley-Davidson and Czechoslovakian Itar, as well as the German Victoria, Aristos, SBD, Mars, Astra and more.

The year 1922 saw the last Tourist Trophy success by a British two-stroke, when Geoff Davison on a Levis won the Lightweight race. It saw also the first double-piston 122cc single-cylinder Puch two-stroke, designed by Giovanni Marcel-lino. Blackburne motorcycle production was taken over by Osborne Engineering Company (OEC), but manufacture of proprietary motorcycle engines continued at Burney & Blackburne. The year also saw the introduction of the first Norton with an ohv engine; Rex Judd rode it at Brooklands. New were Val Page-designed 248cc and 348cc ohc racing engines made by JAP while Hubert Hagens, the British Anzani designer, created the successful 998cc V-twin ohc racing engine, which — ridden by Claude Temple — broke many records.

DKW in Germany built the scooter-like Lomos machine, Walter Handley in 1922 rode his first race on an OK Supreme, Dolf in Germany built an eight-port two-stroke and FN of Belgium entered the market with a 347cc ohv single-cylinder machine. Sheffield-Henderson and Coventry-Victors got saddle-tanks and there was for the first time not only a separate Lightweight TT race, but also the first Ulster GP and

'Lawrence of Arabia' (big picture) owned no less than eight Brough-Superior machines. In the bottom picture, designer and manufacturer George Brough is shown on the left, with business associates and staff, outside his factory in 1927.

at Monza the first Italian Grand Prix. A shaft-driven 498cc Krieger-Gnädig (KG) won the first Avus race at Berlin and a Della Ferrera broke the Italian km record. Interesting, because this works 498cc V-twin had an ohc engine, with chain-driven camshafts; the chains were uncovered and if one takes account of the poor quality of chains in the period, there was a real danger for the rider. This unique design was still seen in 1927 in Italian hill-climbs.

The year 1923 saw the introduction of the first complete 493cc BMW with the transverse-mounted horizontally opposed sv engine, which was already of unit design. This led to the end of proprietary engine production by the Munich factory. Max Friz created the BMW. Less successful than the German factory was Matchless with a new 348cc ohc single, which was never a good racing machine and never really a touring motorcycle either. More interesting was a banking sidecar, used by Freddy Dixon on his Douglas, when winning the 1923 (first ever) sidecar TT race. The same year also saw the first TT race of Amateurs, which eventually became the Manx Grand Prix.

New creations were the A. A. Sidney-designed 348cc ohc Dart and a 398cc BSA prototype, which with its transverse-mounted flat-twin had much in common with the then also new R32 made by BMW. Extremely fast were 144cc and 244cc Hirth two-stroke racers, designed by Helmuth Hirth in Germany. The light-alloy engines were watercooled and of the double-piston variety. Rudge built in 1923 their first ohv models and there was the German Ermag two-stroke, which had a 246cc rotary inlet valve engine, designed by Albert Roder, who created earlier the not unsimilar Ziro. In America, Arthur Lemon took over Henderson design and development from C. Gustafson, while Indian competed for the last time in the Isle of Man TT races. And there was another new TT race; this time in Austria.

The year 1923 was another boom period for motorcycle factories and for manufacturers of proprietary engines as well. The last included the makes JAP, Blackburne, Villiers, Bradshaw, Precision, Coventry-Victor, Broler, Liberty, Dart and on the Continent MAG (Motosacoche), Train, Moser, Zurcher, Chaise, Bekamo, Kühne, Küchen, Baumi, Gruhn, Alba, DKW, Grade etc. A new event in the sporting calendar was the 1000 Mile Stock Trial organised in 1924 by the Auto Cycle Union in England. The year saw also some new designs, including the first ohv BMW model, designed by Rudolf Schleicher, and the new Roconova ohc machines, the first commercially built 248cc and 348cc ohc motorcycles in Germany. Unfortunately Roconova, a design by Johannes Rössig, lasted only three years. In Britain, Connaught bought JES and Brough-Superior introduced Castle forks on the SS100 models, their newest design. Marchant on a Blackburne-engined 348cc Chater-Lea

was the first man officially to break the magic 100 mph limit on a 350cc machine. On April 1, he reached 100·81 mph on a modified 350cc ohc machine. He was a superb designer-tuner as well. Also his friend and opponent Bert le Vack broke records in 1924 and with his 996cc Brough-Superior (ohv JAP) he reached in France over the flying kilometre 119·05 mph, with a one-way run of 122·24 mph. The Americans were fast too and a four-cylinder ACE ridden by Rod Wolverton reached 134 mph. It did not become a world record, as it was not observed officially by the FIM (then still the FICM). The number of registered motorcycles was half a million in England, and British motorcycle exports reached a value of £2,000,000; it was still a period of British supremacy. For Garelli 1924 was a very successful year and the double-piston two-strokes of 348cc won many races against strong opposition. Scott in England was now headed by R. A. Vinter.

Among new machines in 1925 were the 497cc Sunbeam works racers with ohc engines, which never went into quantity production. More successful were the new Italian 348cc Bianchis with double ohc engines, which were nearly unbeatable in Italy until 1931. Velocette in England had a new 348cc ohc single, which was designed by Percy Goodmann and which eventually won races all over the world. New makes were HRD and McEvoy, among others. DKW in Germany produced new water-cooled 173cc racing two-strokes with a charging cylinder at the bottom of the crankcase. The first Dutch TT was run at Assen. A team of very fast 124cc two-stroke singles from Italy won many events. Wal Handley won three 1925 TT races in the Isle of Man in one year. All his machines were made by Rex Acme and had Blackburne ohv engines. In London an unknown young designer named Edward Turner created a 348cc ohc machine; he joined Ariels in 1927 and 10 years later was head of Triumph. George Brough, who built at Nottingham the most expensive machines in England, introduced spring frames. Stefan and Nikolaus v. Horthy, sons of the Hungarian head of state, rode in many races. Among the most enthusiastic motorcyclists was King Albert of Belgium, who got his fifth machine in 1925, a Belgian built Jeecy-Vea with a British engine.

Old William Brough built his last flat-twins in 1926, but his son continued producing the famous Brough-Superiors, including a new 996cc ohv V-twin with the 45 hp JAP engine, for which he guaranteed a top speed of 100 mph (160 km/h). Therefore the name for this model: SS100. Out went the German 5-cylinder Megola, and Paul Kelecom, the famous Belgian designer, left the FN works. Garelli machines broke not less than 48 world records and Chater-Lea built the first 347cc ohc singles with face cams. In Germany, Adolf Brudes broke the German 1 km record with 104 mph on a supercharged 498cc Victoria, designed by Gustav Steinlein. Sepp Stelzer won the big Avus race on a BMW. A new TT race in Czechoslovakia was won by Rupert Karner of Austria on a 497cc ohv double-port Sunbeam, made in England.

Richard Küchen created new 348cc and 498cc face cam ohc proprietary engines, while DKW — then the biggest motorcycle factory in the world — also supplied 124cc, 127cc, 173cc and 206cc two-stroke deflector-type three-port engines to many motorcycle assemblers. Indian and Harley-Davidson still headed motorcycle sales in the USA; Indian with the 596cc Scout, 997cc Chief and 1234cc Big Chief, all side-valve V-twins, and the 348cc single-cylinder Prince. All models were also popular in Europe and Australia. Harley-Davidson built a 348cc sv and ohv single cylinder model in 1926.

The 144cc Austro-Motorette, from the drawing-board of Karl Schüber, was a technically-interesting vertical twin two-stroke machine, made in Austria. Puch added to the 123cc model a 174cc double-piston two-stroke and DSH built a whole range with Villiers and JAP engines. Dunelt now had a 248cc version of the double-diameter piston engine, while FN added a 497cc ohv single to the already existing 347cc ohv single and the big 748cc air-cooled four-in-line. Husqvarna built 548cc and 992cc V-twins with their own sv engines. James had small V-twins with 496cc sv and ohv engines in its wide range.

Equipped with ioe engines, NSU of Germany also had V-twins from 498cc to 996cc and Jock Porter, manufacturer and rider from Edinburgh, still supplied his Blackburne-engined New Gerrards, which brought him many racing successes. A one-model range was introduced by Rudge-Whitworth Ltd. in Coventry. It was a

THE ENGINES OF THE TWENTIES

Make	Bore:	Stroke:	Cubic Capacity:	Cyl	
Alcyon	62	56	174	TS	1
Blackburne	53	79	174	sv	1
	56.2	79	196	sv	1
	63	79	246	sv	1
	69	79	295	sv	1
	69	92	345	sv	1
	81	96.8	498	sv	1
	85	105	598	sv	1
	50	88	173	ohv	1
	56.2	79	196	ohv	1
	60	88	248	ohv	1
	71	88	348	ohv	1
	71	88	348	ohv	1
	71	88	348	ohv	1
	81	96.8	496	ohv	1
	81	96.8	496	ohv	1
	81	96.8	496	ohv	1
	85	105	598	ohv	1
BMW	68	68	493	sv	2
Bradshaw	68	96	349	ohv	1
Coventry-Victor	63	78	499	ohv	2
	69	78	596	sv	2
	75	78	688	sv	2
	78	78	749	ohv	2
DKW	64	64	206	TS	1
	68	68	246	TS	1
Hanfland	55	65	149	TS	1
JAP	60	62	174	sv	1
	55	83	197	sv	1
	64.5	76	248	sv	1
	70	78	299	sv	1
	70	90	345	sv	1
	85.7	85	490	sv	1
	85.7	104	599	sv	1
	70	88	674	sv	2
	70	97	746	sv	2
	85.7	85	976	sv	2
	85.7	85	976	sv	2
	85.7	85	976	sv	2
	53	78	174	ohv	1
	62.5	80	248	ohv	1
	70	90	348	ohv	1
	85.7	85	490	ohv	1
	85.7	104	599	ohv	1
JAP	70	88	674	ohv	2
	74	85	731	ohv	2
	85.7	85	981	ohv	2
Küchen ('K')	70	90	346	sv	1
	79	100	490	sv	1
	70	90	346	ohc	1
	79	100	490	ohc	1
Kühne (Bark)	72	84	342	ohv	1
	84	90	498	sv	1
	84	90	498	ohv	1
MAG (Moto sacoche)	64	77	248	ioe	1
	72	85	346	ioe	1
	82	94	496	ioe	1
	64	77	496	ioe	2
	72	91	741	ioe	2
	82	94	996	ioe	2
	82	103.5	1094	ioe	2
	64	77	248	ohv	1
	72	85	346	ohv	1
	82	94	496	ohv	1
Moser	56	50	124	ohv	1
	60	61	172	ohv	1
Norman Villiers	60	60	170	ohv	1
	50	62	122	TS	1
	55	62	147	TS	1
	57.15	67	172	TS	1
	57.15	67	172	TS	1
	61	67	196	TS	1
	67	70	247	TS	1
	79	70	342	TS	1
Vulpine	78	104	498	ohv	1
	78	104	996	ohv	2

Shown here with his Zenith racing model, designer and rider Bert le Vack broke the world speed record in 1929. Bottom picture: riders in the German Six-Day race of 1927 pose with their Standard machines. This Standard marque was a quality German bike.

498cc four-valve, four-speed ohv single with coupled brakes. Wanderer in Germany had four-valve cylinders too; one model used a V-twin of 708cc and had therefore a total of 8 valves. They also built a flat 196cc single with 4 valves.

A 498cc ohv AJS single, the Douglas sv models — horizontal twins — and a heavy 496cc single-cylinder unit-design D-Rad were among the new creations of 1926. Another was the 498cc V-twin Blackburne ohv racing engine, used in the Senior TT, by Wal Handley and Jock Porter. It was quite fast, but had a tendency to overheat and never went into quantity production. A similar fate befell the MAG ohv V-twins of 498cc and 598cc, as well as works racing V-twins with 748cc. They could be used in short distance events, but overheated in long road races.

Many designers devoted much time and expense to new two-stroke machines. Among them was the Austrian Anton Gazda, who built 248cc motorcycles but became well-known for his Gazda handlebars, consisting of a bundle of leaf springs. An interesting design was the Paramount-Duo, because of its long wheelbase, two very low bucket seats and an enclosed engine supplied by JAP. It was shown at Olympia in London, but was never built in quantity. The Czechoslovakian Böhmerland also had a very long wheelbase and many other interesting technical details. The engine in this case was a 598cc ohv single, designed by Böhmerland boss Albin

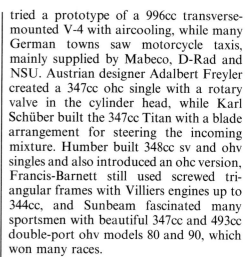

Liebisch. Villiers built a 344cc vertical-twin proprietary two-stroke for the first time, but after a short period it was dropped. A few machines using it were made by Francis-Barnett in England, NSH in Germany, MT in Austria, La Mondiale in Belgium and Monet-Goyon in France.

1927 brought the opening of the Nürburgring, the first 'Cammy' AJS and also the first ohc 490cc Norton, designed by Walter Moore. Indian bought the ACE four, Dougal Marchant joined Motosacoche as designer, and Granville Bradshaw, creator of the ABC, designed the similarly unlucky 247cc Panthette with a transverse-mounted V-twin. Europe's only production version of a 996cc ohc V-twin was a French Koehler-Escoffier, while Windhoff in Germany — where they already built 122cc and 172cc watercooled two-strokes — entered the market with a unique oilcooled 748cc four-cylinder machine with shaft drive. George Brough

tried a prototype of a 996cc transverse-mounted V-4 with aircooling, while many German towns saw motorcycle taxis, mainly supplied by Mabeco, D-Rad and NSU. Austrian designer Adalbert Freyler created a 347cc ohc single with a rotary valve in the cylinder head, while Karl Schüber built the 347cc Titan with a blade arrangement for steering the incoming mixture. Humber built 348cc sv and ohv singles and also introduced an ohc version, Francis-Barnett still used screwed triangular frames with Villiers engines up to 344cc, and Sunbeam fascinated many sportsmen with beautiful 347cc and 493cc double-port ohv models 80 and 90, which won many races.

BSA had a 174cc two-stroke in 1927, Douglas a new 347cc ohv horizontally-opposed twin and there was also a Villiers-engined 172cc NUT, while AKD (Abingdon King Dick) now built 173cc singles with their own ohv engines. There were many factories which switched to saddle tanks, including Ariel, the English Excelsior, Raleigh, New Hudson, James, P&M-Panther, Sun, Coventry-Eagle, Dunelt, Royal-Enfield, Zenith and others. New was the DKW-like 490cc W&G with a nearly vertical twin-cylinder two-stroke engine, but while DKW built this type of machine until the Second World War, the British make soon disappeared.

'Lawrence of Arabia' acquired his fifth Brough-Superior in 1928, FN in Belgium now built 497cc ohv singles, while another Belgian make, Gillet Herstal, had the 348cc Tour de Monde two-stroke single, as well as 498cc ohv singles with their own unit-design engines, and 998cc V-twins with MAG-built ioe engines. In America, the combination of ACE and Indian led to the aircooled 1265cc four-in-line Indian ACE. AJS added a 498cc ohc model to the existing 347cc version of the chain-driven Cammy and Rush, the Belgian make, now built 345cc and 495cc sv and ohv models with their own engines. Moto-Guzzi showed at Milan a spring frame with a 497cc ohv engine and Della Ferrera (not to be confused with Frera) had a new 173cc unit-design ohv model. There was a beautiful production version of the 348cc ohc Bianchi with double ports. And while many experts regarded the English Sunbeam as the nonplus-ultra in motorcycling, it was the Swiss Motosacoche which had this dis-

A rocket-powered motorcycle was tested by Fritz von Opel in 1928. The machine was basically a 496cc Opel Motoclub ohv production model with rockets strapped to the rear end. Soon after this short-lived experiment, Opel stopped making motorcycles.

tinction on the Continent. A new German make, Standard, came very near to Motosacoche as far as quality and finish were concerned.

America had in contrast to Europe only few makes left in 1928: Harley-Davidson, Indian, Super-X, Henderson and Cleveland. DKW was the leading make in Europe. Japan imported machines from England and the USA; their own production was on a very limited scale. The French DFR had a car-type ball gearchange in its four-speed box. The German Neander had a frame made from Duralumin, the BMW new 739cc sv and ohv flat twins, as well as new frames made from pressed steel. BMW works racers got supercharged twins for the 500cc and 750cc classes and Puch of Austria had a new 248cc double-piston two-stroke designed by Giovanni Marcellino. Sturmey-Archer, famous for gearboxes, entered the field with proprietary four-stroke engines from 173cc to 597cc, including a 248cc face-cam ohc version, fitted by Dunelt. Italian factories now built 174cc ohv and ohc models; these included Benelli, Miller, Augusta, Ladetto & Blatto, FVL, Gazzi, Giacomasso, Piana and others.

George William Patchett, ex-McEvoy designer, joined FN and two years later Jawa. Dougal Marchant created very fast 348cc and 498cc ohc racing machines for Motosacoche, with which Walter Handley won the GP of Europe in both classes. England saw the unorthodox Cyril Pullin-designed Ascot-Pullin with a horizontal 497cc ohv single-cylinder engine and OEC introduced duplex steering.

A Rocket-driven Opel motorcycle was tested by Fritz von Opel in Germany, and with Speedway racing coming from Australia to Britain, many factories there — including Douglas, Rudge, Sunbeam, Norton, BSA, James, Calthorpe, Zenith, etc. — built special machines for the sport. Even Scott had such a model. Harley-Davidson came to Europe with such machines, which became known as 'peashooters'.

A new motorcycle factory entered the market in 1929: Jawa of Czechoslovakia. The first model was built under German Wanderer licence. It had a 497cc single-cylinder unit-design ohv engine, a pressed-steel frame and shaft drive. Puch built the first watercooled 248cc works racing two-strokes with double-piston engines and a piston-pump in the crankcase.

Among works machines at Brooklands, Bert Denly rode a 743cc single-cylinder ohc AJS and Bert le Vack a 665cc ohv New Hudson. Germany produced in 1929 195,686 motorcycles, England 164,000. Spanish makes did not appear abroad until after WWII. There was quite a big production in Belgium, with FN, Saroléa, Gillet-Herstal, Rush, La Mondiale, Lady, Ready and a few smaller producers. New in 1929 was a 497cc Harley-Davidson sv single, a 996cc René-Gillet sv V-twin from France and Gillet-Herstal broke 32 world records with the Van Oirbeck-designed 498cc ohc machine. The factory never sold ohc machines and tried everything to hide them from photographers. Even when they had a model called the Record in the catalogue, it had an ohv engine.

We had overhead camshaft engines — like the Velocette, Norton, Chater Lea, AJS— mainly for racing, but other factories including Praga, Chaise, Matchless, Soyer, Dollar etc. also built such power-units in sports models or even touring machines. And when Bert Le Vack broke the world record on August 25, 1929 with 129 mph (208 km/h), his JAP racing V-twin 55 hp engine in its Brough-Superior frame also had overhead valves. New was the five-country Trial in the centre of Europe, but there was a debacle at the International

Six-Day Trial, because of the very bad organisation.

Motosacoche's chief designer Dougal Marchant created a new 248cc single-cylinder ohc racing machine with 27 hp running on alcohol, which was then permitted in road races. 27 hp was for 1929 a superb output by a two-fifty. Interesting also were the four-port 498cc ohv NUT, the 247cc six-port Levis two-stroke, the 494cc watercooled vertical-twin DKW two-strokes, Terrot's square cylinders on the 173cc two-strokes, Sunbeams new saddle tanks, the 493cc ohv Slopers made by BSA and the big 998cc JAP and partly Anzani-engined ohv V-twins produced by Brough-Superior, AJW, Delta-Gnom, Tornax, Ardie, Bücker, Standard, Zenith, OEC and others.

1929 was the year when a 498cc ohv Sunbeam (ridden by Charlie Dodson) won for the last time a Senior TT race and when a 172cc Villiers engine of the Brooklands type in a James frame won the 175cc class in the Belgian Grand Prix, with Bert Kershaw riding. Harley-Davidson introduced a new 746cc sv V-twin, Premier in Czechoslovakia a 498cc long-stroke ohv single and Motobécane of France built a 498cc air-cooled four-in-line.

With the dawn of a new decade, so the era of the entrepreneur-engineer was ending. It had been a golden age.

THE SECOND WORLD WAR

THE MOTORCYCLE saw considerable service in both of the two world wars, but its duties on each occasion were rather different. In the First World War, it had been frequently used by the infantry; in World War Two, it was seen first and foremost as a vehicle of communications, particularly by the Allies. Thus the dispatch rider became one of the war's heroic figures.

About 300,000 American motorcycles were built for World War Two. The bikes were all V-twins. One model, the 500cc Indian, was especially designed for the European war, but this bike was low in power and high in weight. The 750cc Harley 45, on the other hand, was a considerable success. With a top speed of more than 85mph from its racing-trained engine, and the ability to cruise for long distances at high speeds, it out-performed its European contemporaries in road work. It was also successful in the North African campaigns.

The Harley-Davidson company had produced bikes in Japan under the name of Rikuo before the war, then the plant was taken over by the state. Although the Eastern theatres of war rarely had the right terrain for motorcycles, the Japanese Army was equipped with these 'Rikuo' Harleys and they were even used by the Emperor's escort.

The British military motorcycles were mainly medium-weight, 350 singles, with top speeds of little more than 70 mph, capable of good performances both on the road and across country. The Matchless G3L was one of the most popular, with the Ariel NH and the Triumph HRW close behind. Then came the AJS R7, the forerunner of the marque's post-war Grand Prix machine.

The Willys-Ford Jeep did much of the general purpose work which the Axis powers consigned to motorcycle variations. One of the more bizarre among such variations was the tracked motorcycle. This creature was exemplified by the excessively heavy German 'Kettenkrad', made by NSU and powered by a 1·5 litre Opel engine.

A simpler and more effective approach was found in the development of motorcycle combinations with sidecar-wheel drive. The Belgian FN factory launched a 1,000cc flat-twin series, the M12, in 1934 for Service use. This was essentially a tricycle, driving on the two rear wheels, which could be fitted with a differential gear. FN chose to drop the tricycle layout in favour of a conventional combination when they produced a heavily-armoured version, the M86, in which the sidecar wheel was driven but had no differential. The usefulness of this machine was destroyed by its great and badly distributed weight.

The Germans took over the FN factory once they occupied Belgium. In France, they were also impressed by the Gnome-Rhône combination, which had sidecar-wheel drive but no differential. When the German Forces needed a new outfit to replace the BMW R12 motorcycle combination, the FN and Gnome & Rhône combinations were available for study, and the project was given to BMW and Zündapp. The resulting BMW R75 with an overhead-valve engine could reach 55 mph with a three-man crew and full loading, and had remarkable off-road performance, only exceeded by the new Zündapp KS.

Zündapp then introduced the differential gear, which was unique on a conventional combination. The gear did not split power equally between the two driving wheels, but shared torque according to the centre of gravity between them. BMW shared this system, along with numerous other components, such as electrical and carburation equipment. These outfits were very effective, though they were costly and complicated to build and could not be manufactured quickly enough.

The Italians placed their faith in the solo machine with a classic Moto-Guzzi, the Alce, the forerunner of today's uprated Falconi. The Alce was a beautifully designed bike: its top speed was 80 mph, and the forward facing horizontal layout of its 500cc engine contributed to a weight distribution which helped stability and manoeuvrability. An Alce was produced with a machine-gun mounted on the handlebars, and an additional pair of dummy handlebars for the pillion passenger to support the bike while the driver used the gun. Alternatively the pillion passenger could lean over and fire the gun while the driver supported the bike. Predictably neither of these methods proved very

Military requirements led to a variety of special design. The U.S. Army used Harley-Davidson 45 WLAs (facing page) with a holster for a submachine gun. The British experimented with attachments for a mortar and a submachine gun (big picture) on Norton motorcycles. The Germans tried a scooter for paratroops, and a tracked vehicle, the NSU HK101 Kettenkrad.

practicable for safe and effective use.

Gilera manufactured a 500cc single, which was notable for the use of both side and over-head valves within the same engine, and Bianchi and Sertim produced more conventional side-valve 500cc models. All three were frequently fitted with side-cars.

As the portability, reliability and range of radio improved, and other means of communication developed, the military usefulness of the motorcycle faded from immediate view. Nor in the post-war period would motorcycling ever quite recover its former colour, though the British Corgi and American Cushman 'parascooters' briefly brought a minuscule new dimension to two-wheel riding, and the Piaggi aircraft company developed the Vespa scooter.

Many different manufacturers supplied machines for military use. American M.P.s used the Harley-Davidson; BMW supplied their R35 (below) and R75 (right). Bottom: BSA were one of the major British suppliers, making both 350 and 500cc models. The Indian soldier is reclining on a Matchless G3/L, a 350cc ohv machine.

THE GREAT DESIGNERS

The most famous and successful motorcycles have been designs so good that they have been produced for many years with a minimum of modernization and development.

Adalberto Garelli designed his first double-piston two-strokes before 1914; they continued to be developed until 1935. J. L. Norton designed the Norton sv singles which won so many races; as a normal production version, the 16H was in the catalogue for many years and was made in thousands for the military during the Second World War. The Austrian Puch machines had a very long run; designed by Giovanni Marcellino in 1923, they were made until the 1960s. Marcellino's masterpieces were works racing machines having 248cc watercooled engines with pumping pistons in the crankcase. At the German Grand Prix in 1931, they beat everything in sight. Not all designers stayed with one

company. Edward Turner had joined Ariel in 1927; his 1930 Ariel square four was a big success. In 1936 he took over Triumph on behalf of its new owner, Jack Sangster; the next year he built Triumph's first 498cc vertical twin, the Speed Twin, by fitting the engine into an existing frame from a single-cylinder model. It was an instant success. There had been two previous Triumph vertical twins: a 448cc prototype in 1913, and a 649cc ohv unit-design model designed by Val Page in 1933, which was marketed at a time when few buyers could afford such a big machine. Page was a very good designer who had worked for years on JAP proprietary engines, but the 1937 Triumph vertical twin was a perfect example of the right design at the right time; it was the first commercially successful vertical twin, and inspired a great many others.

Famous designer George William Pat-

chett joined Jawa in Prague, after being with George Brough, Michael McEvoy and the FN works. His designs for Jawa included two machines—a 173cc and a 246cc two-stroke with pressed steel frames, and 346cc sv and ohv singles. There were also 247cc two-strokes with Auto-Union (Schnürle patent) flat-top engines.

Harold Willis designed the Roarer for Velocette in 1939; this was a supercharged vertical twin ohc with 498cc and shaft drive. The war and Willis's death prevented racing of the machine. After the war, Charles Udall was responsible for the silent watercooled Velocette LE, with a 198cc transverse-mounted flat twin, in connection with Percy and Bertie Goodmann.

In the 1920s Richard Küchen designed the famous 3-valve 'K' series of proprietary engines; in the 1930s, he was responsible

The famous British designer Bradshaw began his career with the ABC in 1913

The designs created by Marcellino (centre) for Puch lasted from the 1920s to the 1960s

D. R. O'Donovan (on bike) . . . Norton genius

Creator of the Speed Twin . . . Edward Turner (standing directly behind the fuel tank)

W. W. Moore (left), of Norton and NSU . . . and George William Patchett, of Jawa

for sv and ohv engines as well. In 1933, he created the Zündapp range, with pressed steel frames and two and four-stroke engines from 198 to 798cc. The biggest was a transverse-mounted flat four, and many models had shaft drive. After the Second World War, Küchen designed Opti vertical twin ohc proprietary engines, double-piston two-strokes and even racing car engines. His engines were always of clean design, but their finesse was often the work of his lesser-known brother, Xaver.

Between the wars, George Brough continued to construct the most expensive motorcycles in the world, but he never built his own engines, using MAG, JAP and Matchless units. In 1932 be built 796cc models with two rear wheels, and they had watercooled Austin car engines. Some prototypes had engine parts made by Motosacoche; among these was the Dream, with a 996cc transverse-mounted flat-four.

An outstanding design of 1935 was the AJS 499cc double-ohc V-four, which was the work of Bert Collier. It was afterwards modified to watercooling and also supercharged in 1939, and was the fastest pre-war British road racer of its size.

W. W. Moore had designed the first Norton ohc machine in 1927. In 1930 he joined the German NSU works and created the not dissimilar 490cc single. His work at Norton was taken over by Arthur Carroll, while Irishman Joe Craig took over development and team management. Carroll redesigned the camshaft arrangement and made the Nortons faster and more reliable before his death in an accident in 1935. (From 1950 onwards, Norton machines had the superb featherbed frame, the Irish invention of Rex and Crommie McCandless and Artie Bell.)

After World War II, German Victoria had the 198cc 'Swing', a swinging arm two-stroke designed by Norbert Riedel. In 1948 Riedel designed the very unorthodox Imme, a 98cc two-stroke with a one-sided fork and the engine on the swinging arm. Sunbeams designed after the war by Ealing Poppe were entirely different machines from the pre-war models, with 498cc vertical-twin ohc in-line engines and shaft drive. Vincenz Sklenar designed 348 and 498cc double-ohc racing twins right after the war; Jaroslav Walter created 248 and 348cc ohc singles for CZ after 1949. When MV-Agusta entered racing in the early 1950s, the 498cc four was designed by Piero Remor.

Among today's designers, Mario Sucher is responsible for Austrian Puch machines, Walter Kaaden for MZ two-strokes, and Jörg Möller of West Germany designed the very fast Italian Morbidellis. Alan Clough's CCM moto-cross four-strokes are still among the leaders in their class.

Crommie McCandless ... of featherbed fame

Remor (left) with Gilera

Val Page ... of JAP and Triumph renown

Fabio Taglioni (above) designed the Ducati desmodromic valve gear in the early 1960s. The system is still in use. Right: Giulio Carcano with Moto-Guzzi Junior TT winner in 1956.

Jack Williams, chief development engineer on the AJS 7R, with son-in-law Tom Herron, of Yamaha

Pioneer Max Friz ... he made aircraft engines, then the first BMW motorcycle

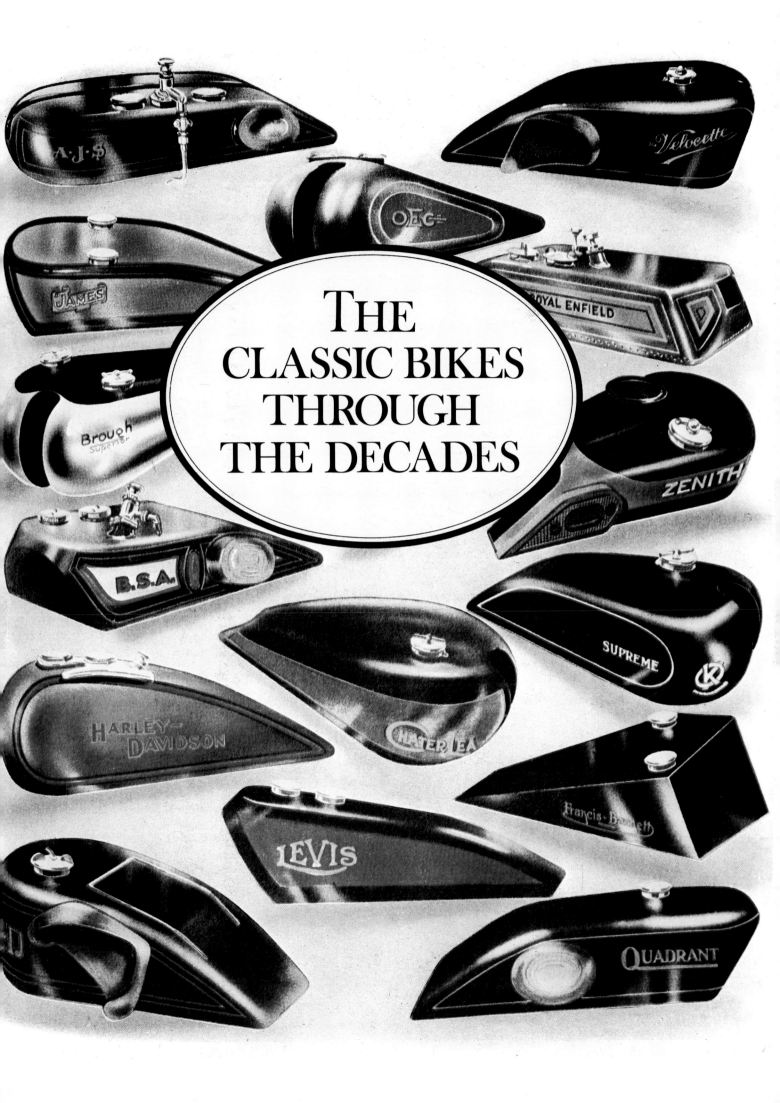

THE CLASSIC BIKES THROUGH THE DECADES

NO FOUR-CYLINDER MOTORCYCLE has achieved such pre-eminence in its own time as the Henderson. It provided riders in the early years of motorcycling with simple starting, smoothness, silence, oil tightness, reliability and generous power to a degree unmatched elsewhere. The model shown here is that of 1912, the first year of production. The original 7 hp model was soon further developed, with a multi-speed gearbox, improved power, and and more robust construction. Sales rose accordingly, and the model achieved greater popularity than any comparable machine in the United States. Finally, Ignaz Schwinn's Excelsior Company bought the firm in 1917, initially retaining the services of founders William and Tom

Henderson. After that, the Henderson big four also incorporated the name Excelsior on the tank. Two years later, William and Tom Henderson left Excelsior, unhappy with the new business arrangement. William founded his own motorcycle company, under the name of Ace. He was soon manufacturing an Ace four, and challenging the Henderson's reputation for quality. After many successful years Ace ran into financial troubles, and was bought by Indian.

988 F

THE NAME SCOTT is central to the history of the motorcycle. Alfred Scott was an inventor and engine-designer who played a leading part in the development of the two-stroke machine. Scott built his first motorised bicycle in Yorkshire as early as 1898, using a twin-cylinder two-stroke. The engine was fitted to a heavy pedal-cycle, and transmission was by friction roller. By 1903, he had built a machine with rear-wheel power, and a year later Scott was granted British patent rights on a two-stroke vertical-twin engine. Scott's first true production motorcycle was manufactured in 1908. Its engine was built to the Scott design by the nearby Jowett car factory, another Yorkshire concern famous in automotive history. This 333cc engine had a bore and stroke of 58 × 63mm, and the entire unit weighed only 371 lbs. The cylinder heads were water-cooled through a thermosiphon system, but the barrels were air-cooled. By 1914, Scott had settled the design of his machines, and was using a wholly water-cooled engine. The two-speed machine had standard gear-ratios of 3:1 and 4:1, and the unusual "open" frame design which characterised the marque. This frame design was popular with women motorcyclists, whose dignity it helped preserve. Telescopic front forks were used from the very first, and a disc-valve induction and exhaust system was introduced at an early stage. Other machines could match the Scott's 55 mph top speed, but none of its contemporaries offered the same handling qualities. It was this characteristic in particular which afforded Scott such great racing success. Like most unconventional machines, the Scott was the creature of its designer. Alfred Scott himself left the company after the First World War, and died in 1923; within four or five years, the marque had lost much of its shine. Production since a takeover in 1950 has been limited to small-scale revivals. The Scott shown here is a 486cc model specially reconstructed for vintage racing.

INDIAN WAS WITHOUT DOUBT one of the foremost names in the development of the modern motorcycle. In 1905, the factory became one of the first to put a V-twin into commercial manufacture. The first V engine was little more than a doubling up of two Indian 1·75 hp singles, but improved and enlarged versions soon followed. These ultimately provided the basis for the very advanced motorcycles produced under the aegis of the factory's founder, George Hendee, and the great designer Oskar Hedström. After they had left the company, Charlie Gustafson became Indian's chief designer in 1915. He established the side-valve style which became a tradition of the factory and of the American motorcycle industry. His great machine

was the 7 hp 998 cc Power Plus shown here. This sophisticated and speedy motorcycle included such advanced equipment as leaf-spring suspended pivoted fork rear suspension, all chain drive, electric lighting, electric starting and a proper kick-start.

Indian

EL 5172

AS THE ORIGINAL William Brough motorcycle company entered the last year of its life, the son's rival firm launched the most famous machine to bear the family name. The Brough Superior SS100, introduced in 1926, was more popular than any other prestige sports roadster before or since. The SS100, shown here, was an overhead-valve V-twin. It became one of the two mainstays of Brough Superior's 16-year production period, along with its predecessor, the SS80 side-valve V-twin. As with all engines of its type, the side-valve twin was less durable at speed than the ohv. The '100' and '80' model designations referred to the machines' guaranteed top speed. Brough Superior was also known for a proliferation of multi-cylindered exotica.

The machines were largely assembled from proprietary components—the engines were principally JAP or Matchless units, and even the famous Castle forks were originally a Harley Davidson design. This philosophy was the Achilles' heel of Brough Superior.

The company tried unsuccessfully to develop its own power-units, and the cost of buying-in specially-manufactured engines in small quantities eventually proved to be crippling. The company went out of business in 1938.

Brough Superior

SUNBEAM

THE SUNBEAM MODEL 90, shown on the right in its traditional black-and-gold livery, is probably the finest example of British single-cylinder engineering. It used simple, proven designs, with meticulous finish. The machine was conceived in 1923 as a sports roadster, and successfully adapted as a works racer. It was produced in both 350 and 500cc ohv versions. Production standards dropped after the factory was bought in 1930 by ICI (Imperial Chemical Industries). Sunbeam was later owned by Associated Motorcycles and BSA.

Douglas

ALTHOUGH DOUGLAS did sometimes use other engine layouts, the marque was always known for its horizontally-opposed twins. Today, Douglas is usually remembered for its post-war series of transverse-engined 350cc machines, but these were only made in the company's last seven years. In its earlier days, and for more than three decades, Douglas found its fame and fortune in exceptionally well-planned twins with a fore-and-aft arrangement. The success of these machines owed much to the work of the company's chief development rider, Freddie Dixon, during the middle and late 1920s. Fate also played a part. When the Douglas EW series of 350sv racers began to find the competition tough, Douglas had planned a new ohc model, but a fire at the works destroyed the blueprints and set back the company's work. The new engine was abandoned, and the company chose instead to give a new life to its old ohv twins, with considerable development work by Dixon. By happy chance, these machines proved most successful in the newly-arrived sport of speedway. Some of their success was due to a freak of design which led the frame to flex during broadsliding, but their achievements on the cinder track boosted all aspects of the Douglas reputation. During this period, the classic Douglas machine was the model FW, which was produced in 500cc and 600cc versions. The road-racing version is shown here. The road-racing models were capable of 90 mph and 95 mph respectively. In 1929 alone, 1300 machines were sold.

Rudge

SOME OF THE BEST British production bikes were replicas of their makers' works racing models. A fine example was the 1929 Rudge-Whitworth Ulster, which came from a factory famous for its advanced approach. The machine was introduced to celebrate Graham Walker's win in the Ulster Grand Prix, and it proved to be exceptionally fast and reliable. It had a four-speed positive-stop, foot-change gearbox, dry sump lubrication with a mechanical pump, and a four-valve cylinder head in a penthouse combustion chamber.

THE BRITISH EXCELSIOR company is remembered with affection for a 250cc single which was popularly known as the "Mechanical Marvel," but this four-valve ohv machine suffered from its own complexity. Undaunted, Excelsior continued along the same development path with an improved four-valver, the famous Manxman, shown here. This machine had a single overhead camshaft, and each inlet valve was fed by its own Amal RN carburettor. The bronze head, as shown, improved thermal efficiency in the days before aluminium had come into common use. The Manxman shown is a 250, but a 350 was also produced. Valve gear and carburettor tune still proved "very pernickerty" according to Excelsior's managing director Eric Walker, and in 1938 the firm introduced two-valve engines. These were equally fast, but wholly reliable. They had sprung frames, and proved so successful that they continued to be raced in private hands into the early 1950s.

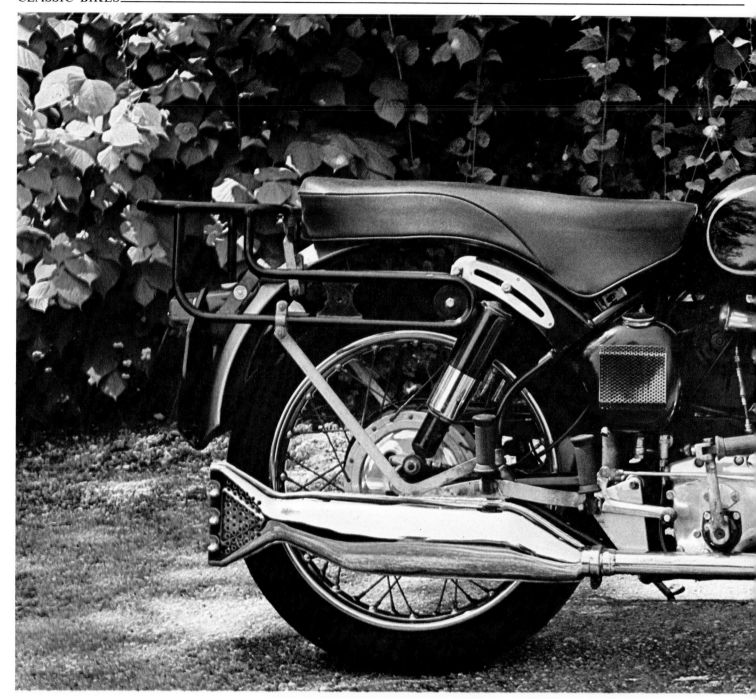

Velocette

OTHER SINGLE-CYLINDER machines may have exemplified a particular aspect of engineering or of performance, but those produced by Velocette demonstrated the full range of attributes. This was best accomplished by the KTT (left), a racing replica of the works' own grand prix machinery, which was also notable as the first model to sport the Velocette-perfected foot gear-change system. This was an ohc

single of 350cc, sold with a guaranteed top speed of 85 mph. As an option, Velocette offered a 100 mph dope-tuned model sporting a 9:1 compression ratio. The range ran from the 1929 Mk 1 illustrated here to the 1949 Mk VIII. In 1956, Velocette demonstrated its skills with a quite different range of well-remembered singles. These were ohv sports roadsters. First came the 499cc Venom, shown above, with a "square" (86 × 86mm) engine, then the smaller 349cc Viper. The Venom engine developed 36 bhp at 6,200 rpm, giving the machine a top speed of 95 mph. After 12 and 24-hour records had been set at Montlhéry, a highly-tuned version was produced as a clubman racer. This was the Thruxton (right), which had a top speed of approximately 120 mph.

BSA

FOR MOST OF ITS LIFE, the BSA marque was known primarily for singles of simple and inexpensive design, made for everyday transport. The motorcycles in the small picture are examples: a 250cc machine from 1925 (background) and the 1928 "Sloper". In later years, the same qualities of durability and reliability were showcased in a much more exotic motorcycle, the Gold Star. No clubman racer has ever enjoyed the success or reputation of the "Goldie". The range was produced in trial, scramble, touring and racing versions, and a 1959 model of the latter is shown here. The 500cc engine developed up to 40 bhp at just over 7,000 rpm, through a close ratio gearbox. Top speed was around 120 mph in full clubman trim.

HARLEY-DAVIDSON

THE HARLEY-DAVIDSON Electra-Glide has its origins in the SV 74 twin of 1922, although its more recent and direct ancestor is the first ohv 1200 of 1941. These early machines displayed the familiar styling features of most American motorcycles: leading link front forks, solid rear wheel mounting, pan saddles, footboards, high, wide handle-bars, and a V-twin engine, all of which produce comfort at low cruising speeds. Over the years, the range has been modernised and renamed, but the essential concept has remained the same. In 1949, the Hydra-Glide was introduced with a telescopic front fork. The next model, with pivoted-fork rear suspension, produced in 1959, was the Duo-Glide. With the addition of a starter motor in 1965 came the name Electra-Glide. Since then, little has changed except the adoption of cast alloy wheels, although numerous Japanese components, such as forks and carburettor, have been adopted. The Electra-Glide is the heaviest mass-produced motorcycle ever built, weighing 800 lbs fully equipped. The 45°, 1207cc V-twin has hydraulically-activated push-rods and produces 62 bhp at 5,200 rpm, and 70ft/lbs of torque at 4,000 rpm. For all its cumbrous luxury, the Harley has a speedy history. In the 1920s, when the marque was locked in competition with Indian, sporting feats were constantly being publicised. In 1920, several new times were set over a kilometre at Daytona. Harley, which was already well known in Britain, also made several celebrated runs at Brooklands. The 1,200cc machine shown below broke the Flying Kilometre record in 1923, at 108·6 mph, in the hands of the famous British rider Freddie Dixon.

THERE ARE MANY REASONS for celebrating the famous marque founded by Howard R. Davies (hence its original name, HRD) and bought shortly afterwards by Philip Vincent. Modern motorcycle manufacturers have still barely caught up with the progressive chassis-group designs produced by Vincent 35 years ago, though the marque is more commonly remembered for its spree of speedy achievement during the 1950s. Perhaps these sporting feats were the inspiration for the unusually-large and ambitious speedo which was fitted to Vincent motorcycles. Factory and private riders captured national and world speed and sprint records by the

handful on the competition model of the period, the Black Lightning. The word "Black" featured in the names of several famous Vincent machines. One unsupercharged Black Lightning achieved a speed of 185·15 mph in the hands of Russell Wright, a New Zealander, in 1955. Sadly, this was also the last year of full production.

The firm went out in a blaze of glory, with the announcement of the semi-streamlined Series D models, but few were actually made. In design, these machines were the natural successors to the Series C Rapides, which had been launched in 1949, with 50-degree 998cc V-twin engines. The Series C standard touring machine provided a top speed of approximately 105/110 mph, and its sporting counterpart the Black Shadow (shown here) went to 110/120 mph, reaching 56 mph in only six seconds. These machines were in turn developed from the Series A Rapides, which were launched in 1937, had 47-degree engines, and had a web of external pipes.

ARIEL was in every sense an historic British marque. Established since 1898, the firm exhibited all the characteristics of British motorcycle manufacture. The products were well made, even sporty, but initially of conventional design. In 1929, a much more sophisticated machine made a considerable break with tradition. This was a 500cc four with a highly-unusual "square" cylinder configuration and single overhead camshaft. This distinctive engine layout became so identifiable with the marque that the nickname "Squariel" passed into the language of motorcycling. Like the later Triumph Speed Twin, another pace-setting machine, the Square

Four was designed by Edward Turner. It had an all ball-and-roller bearing engine and horizontally-split crankcase. In 1931, the engine was bored out from 51 to 56 mm, thus increasing capacity to 600cc. Although some modest success was achieved in competition, such as the Bickel

brothers' supercharged 111·42 lap at Brooklands in 1934, the machine was really a sporting tourer. In 1936, Ariel launched a 1,000cc Square Four of quite new engine design. This model had a pushrod power-unit, with plain bearings, and it also utilised a unique trailing-link rear-suspension system. It remained in production in various roadster forms until the late 1950s, by which time it boasted four individual exhaust-pipes ports and an all-aluminium engine. The 1956 luxury roadster shown here develops 42 bhp at 5,800 rpm, providing a top speed of 105 mph. It has a bore and stroke of 65 × 75 mm. The machine's kerb-weight is 495 lbs.

TRIUMPH WILL ALWAYS be associated with the vertical-twin engine-layout. This classic design was introduced in 1938, in the 498cc Speed Twin, which was the fore-runner of many famous motorcycles. A memorable example was the larger Thunderbird (above), introduced in 1949. This 649cc tourer produced 34 bhp at 6,000 rpm on a compression ratio of 7:1. Three standard models averaged 101·06 mph between them for 500 miles at Montlhéry. A total break with the vertical-twin layout came in the 1960s with the transverse three-cylinder Trident (left), which had an ohv 740cc engine of 67 × 70 mm bore and stroke, developing 58 bhp at 7,500–8,000 rpm. This machine had a top speed of more than 125 mph.

Norton

IT WAS THE GREAT racing success of the Norton marque which created the need for an improved frame in the 1940s. The need was met by the McCandless brothers' Featherbed frame, which in turn influenced motorcycle design almost everywhere. After being introduced on the Manx racers, the Featherbed frame was modified for road use in the existing 497cc tourer, which became the Dominator in 1952. The example shown above was made a year later. Ten years after its launch, the Dominator had grown to 647cc, with a maximum road speed of 112 mph. In 1965, Norton launched the 745cc Atlas, but a more significant development came two years later. The same engine was fitted, with rubber mountings, into a new duplex frame. This new model, the Commando, was subsequently increased in size to 828cc. With a top speed of 120 mph, the Commando (left) is the most powerful road-going Norton ever produced.

LIKE THE LAMBORGHINI CAR, the equally exotic Laverda motorcycle is the product of an Italian agricultural engineering group. With a speed of 150 mph, verified in independent tests, the Laverda "Jota" is by far the fastest production roadster ever made. The Jota was developed in a collaboration between the factory and the British concessionaire. The standard 981cc dohc Laverda shown here still manages a tidy 130 mph, and develops 80 bhp at 8,000 rpm.

THE MV AGUSTA AMERICA is arguably the finest sports roadster in production, and without doubt a classic among the multi-cylindered big bikes. The entire power-unit is a development of the company's racing 500cc four of the 1950s. MV was the last European marque to dominate the Grand Prix circuits, and retired solely for commercial reasons, but it took several attempts before the factory's sporting experience could be translated into a successful roadster. The 788cc dohc America develops 75 bhp at 8,500 rpm, and its top speed is approximately 135 mph.

MOTO GUZZI

WHILE JAPANESE motorcycles have become increasingly sophisticated, the largest of the Italian manufacturers has responded by offering machines of comparable performance but robust simplicity. The V 850 GT of 1972 typifies Moto Guzzi's approach. The transverse twin turns out 64·5 bhp at a mere 6,500 rpm, providing a top speed of 115 mph. In 1975, the entire range was expanded to include the revolutionary V 1,000, with hydraulic torque converter.

DUCATI

IT WAS BUILT for its high-speed handling, apparently with no other priority in mind, and in this respect the Ducati Desmo 864cc of 1975 has no serious rival. Its top speed is 135 mph, its kerb weight a mere 428 lbs, and it is a remarkably stable motorcycle. The machine also benefits from the efficiency and reliability of the desmodromic valve system. Only Ducati has used this system with total success. The technique was employed to great effect in the 1972 750 SS clubman racer, after being first introduced by the factory's chief engineer, Fabioni Taglioni, in the successful Grand Prix period which was during the late 1950s.

THERE HAS NEVER BEEN a more aero-dynamically advanced motorcycle than the BMW R100/RS. Nor has there been a simpler, more practical machine within this class of motorcycle. The horizontally-opposed 980cc ohv twin produces 70 bhp at 7,250 rpm (DIN), and a top speed of more than 125 mph. This performance can be achieved without any special effort or skill on the part of the rider. Furthermore, the rider is protected from the weather by a pocket of still air, thanks to a fairing developed in the Pinin Farina wind tunnel in Milan. The fairing also improves penetration by 5·4 per cent, negates front-wheel lift, and increases downward pressure by 17·4 per cent. Lateral stability in particular is improved by 60 per cent.

These benefits were brought about by designer Hans Muth, whose background in car styling taught him how to utilise the wind, rather than fighting it. The dimensions and shape of the seat were also evolved with aerodynamic requirements in mind. The cockpit layout is in the sports car idiom, and the rider is even equipped with voltmeter and electric clock. The R100 weighs 530 lbs equipped for the road, and will cover a quarter-mile sprint in 13·5 seconds.

IT WAS WITH the racing success of machines like the 1960 Honda 250 four (small picture) that the Japanese motorcycle industry first claimed the attention of the Western world. When the sophisticated Gold Wing was launched in 1974, it met with some scepticism, but its elaborate design soon proved itself. The horizontally-opposed transverse four-cylinder layout makes for smooth running; the water-cooling improves the mechanical silencing and temperature control; shaft-drive affords longevity in the transmission; a low centre of gravity is achieved by the positions of the gearbox (beneath the engine) and the 4·2-gallon tank (beneath the seat nose); the dummy tank above the engine neatly and accessibly contains the

coolant header tank, the majority of ancillary electrical components, tools, and emergency crank. Unusually, in a shaft driven motorcycle, the countershaft-mounted clutch is of the wet, multi-plate type. A contra-rotating generator along-side it successfully counteracts the lateral torque effect inherent in "flat"-engined machinery. At 6,500 rpm, torque amounts to 60ft/lbs, and at 7,500 rpm, the engine develops a DIN-rated 84 bhp. Top speed is more than 120 mph.

⚡ SUZUKI

WHEN SUZUKI LAUNCHED the first mass-produced rotary-engine motorcycle in 1975, the company took a calculated risk The success or failure of the Suzuki RE5 hinged on a paradox: the well-known selling-point of the rotary engine was its fundamental simplicity, yet precisely this advantage was seriously challenged by the complexity of the ancillary parts which it required. The engine of the RE5 demands two separate cooling systems, one using water and the other oil, and each with its own radiator. While the unusually-hot combustion area of the unit needs cooling, the induction side needs warming, for which purpose the same water is circulated. Such convoluted engineering has to be monitored with an instrument panel which contains a total of ten warning systems. Although it is rated as a 500cc engine, the power-unit has three chambers of this size, thus making for a large motorcycle. At 550 lbs, it is equal in weight to a conventional 750cc machine. Top speed is approximately 112 mph; there is no vibration; and the power-band is broader than that of any conventional motorcycle. Maximum torque of 54·9 ft/lbs is developed at 3,600 rpm, and 62 bhp at 7,000 rpm. Ignition is by transistorised capacitator discharge, incorporating carburettor sensors for advance and retard operation. The engineering and constructional skills used in the development of the RE5 were quite exceptional, and for them the machine wins a place in the history of the motorcycle, whatever the future of the rotary engine.

✹ YAMAHA

IF ANTI-POLLUTION LAWS and the cost of fuel prevent the further development of the two-stroke engine in full-size roadsters, the Yamaha twins will be remembered as the last of the line. These machines have probably the most efficient two-stroke roadster engines ever made. The 398cc RD400 shown here develops 40 bhp at 7,000 rpm, and its powerful mid-range torque development provides impressive acceleration, with a top speed of more than 100 mph. The combustion efficiency is attributable to reed-valve controlled carburation and an extra, seventh-port induction system. It had a six-speed gearbox and very powerful brakes.

Kawasaki

THREE-CYLINDER TWO STROKES had been made before, but none so deliberately aimed at massive power and speed as the 1969 Kawasaki H1 Mach III, a 498cc transverse three. From an unusually weak torque development below 6,000 rpm, the engine roused itself at 7,000 to produce 42·3ft/lbs, and at 7,500 a DIN-rated 60 bhp. Top speed was approximately 120 mph, and a quarter-mile sprint resulted in a time of little more than 12 seconds. Unfortunately, the design of the cycle parts was less successful, and the machine's mighty performance proved difficult to handle. The engine was progressively de-tuned in later years until it faded out in 1974.